MACHINE MAGIC

DEBORAH LOUIE

Get the Most from the Decorative Stitches on Your Sewing Machine • 22 Fun Flowers to Sew

C&T PUBLISHING

Text and photography copyright © 2022 by Deborah Louie

Photography and artwork copyright © 2022 by C&T Publishing, Inc.

Publisher: Amy Barrett-Daffin

Creative Director: Gailen Runge

Acquisitions Editor: Roxane Cerda

Managing Editor: Liz Aneloski

Editor: Karla Menaugh

Technical Editor: Debbie Rodgers

Cover/Book Designer: April Mostek

Production Coordinator: Tim Manibusan

Production Editor: Jennifer Warren

Illustrator: Aliza Shalit

Photography Coordinator: Lauren Herberg

Photography Assistant: Gabriel Martinez

Instructional and subjects photography by Estefany Gonzalez; lifestyle photography by Tristan Gallagher of C&T Publishing, Inc., unless otherwise noted

Published by C&T Publishing, Inc., P.O. Box 1456, Lafayette, CA 94549

Library of Congress Control Number: 2021945640

Printed in the USA

10 9 8 7 6 5 4 3 2

Dedication

To my family—past, present, and future—who are always with me stitch by stitch in every quilt.

Acknowledgments

This book was written through the months of COVID-19 isolation in my home at Oyster Bay, Sydney, in 2021. I took solace in the rhythm of my sewing machine, stitch after stitch, pattern after stitch pattern, and I was inspired by the intense bright colors of fabrics that lifted my spirits during a difficult time for the world.

I acknowledge with heartfelt thanks my first quilting teacher, the late Coral Garnsey. Little did she know what she started! My sincere thanks also go to my dear friend Denise Green for all she has done for me over the years. To Jan Browne, thank you for all of your guidance, support, and friendship.

To Pauline Rogers, thank you for your support and for introducing me to C&T Publishing, who helped me fulfill a dream in writing this book.

Thank you also to Greg Alexander and Kerrie Hay of BERNINA Australia for your support over the years and for the beautiful sewing machines used to create my projects.

My thanks go to my past and present students from quilt shops, guilds, symposiums, retreats, and workshops for the trust you placed in me to guide you over the years in quilting the Deborah Louie way.

A special thanks to my Friday Princesses for your friendship and inspiring me to keep moving forward.

I am blessed with so many special friends—thank you for your friendship, for your company when I am away from home, and for continuing to inspire me with your passion for quiltmaking.

To my parents, thank you for giving me a strong work ethic. My early memories of the Luton Dye Works with the colors of the dyes and the beautiful laces will remain in my heart forever. To my extended family and friends, thanks for the use of your names on the flowers and leaves in this book. Your encouragement and support of my work means so much.

To my childhood school friends, the champagne 6, thank you for your ongoing friendship and love.

To my dear sister, who is always there no matter what the circumstances are, thank you. To those who I love the most, my children and their partners, thank you for being there, for the support of my passion for quiltmaking, and for supporting each other while I was often away from home teaching. Your love, counselling, and opinions when I was at a crossroads with a quilt always means so much. I love you all from the bottom of my heart.

Most importantly, to my best friend, my husband, your unconditional love and compassion lifts me every day to strive further, do better, be more, and love more. Thank you. I love you.

Only you.

CONTENTS

Doreen's Place Mat   98

Little Garden Cushion   104

Bigger Garden Cushion 112

Garden Runner 120

WELCOME TO A GARDEN OF DECORATIVE-STITCH APPLIQUÉ

I *adore the texture that machine appliqué can bring to my quilts. I'm excited about the use of different weights and types of threads, as well as the hundreds of decorative stitches on my sewing machine. I hope to share my love and excitement of the sewing machine with you, irrespective of the brand or model you have. All sewing machines offer fabulous opportunities to add magic to your appliqué quilts.*

In these projects, you will find a family of beautiful flowers, leaves, and clamshells that are all hand drawn. All are named after people dear to me. You will become very familiar with the step-by-step instructions shown in the flowers named Doreen and Eileen. There are four projects—a place mat, a small cushion, a stunning large European-sized cushion, and the masterpiece: a table or bed runner to enhance any home decor.

I have made many award-winning appliqué quilts based on flower designs. Growing up in Sydney, Australia, I spent many hours playing in a garden filled with dahlias, hibiscus, daisies, and roses. These are the flowers I chose to base my projects on for this book.

As a quilt tutor, I strive to educate each student, from the beginner to advanced quilter, to have a passion for their machines and its wonderful features. I encourage you to explore the many features of your machine, including stitch length, width, mirror reverse, elongation, stitch density, and many more. I will guide you through each process—for example, how to design for machine appliqué, how to set up your machine, and how to use different weights and types of threads for stunning results. I will also explain how to solve tension difficulties, thread breakages, and starting and finishing a stitch pattern neatly.

In my unique machine-appliqué technique, every flower is constructed separately by fusing its appliqué shapes together in either one of two methods—the Stacking Technique or the Layering Technique. Stabilizer is pinned to the constructed flower and the decorative stitch patterns are then stitched inside the appliqué, which makes it so much easier to handle. After the decoratively stitched flower is pressed onto the background fabric, it is completed with sketch-edge appliqué. Watch how your constructed flower comes to life with stunning, textural decorative stitch patterns!

The machine quilting in all the projects is just as important as the appliqué techniques. No quilt-as-desired instructions here. I explain the beauty of ditch-quilting appliqué to highlight the stitch patterns. Learn the background walking foot and free-motion quilting for all the projects.

You will find step-by-step instructions and photos for all machine appliqué and machine-quilting techniques. I hope you will be thrilled with your finished projects and the increased knowledge of your sewing machine you will have gained.

—Deborah

PLANNING YOUR
DECORATIVE-
STITCH PROJECT

EXPLORING THE BEAUTY OF MACHINE APPLIQUÉ

Why Use Decorative Stitches to Machine Appliqué?

Today's sewing machines are computers and have the most wonderful features. These features save us time, ensure our stitching looks perfect, and give us the opportunity to be as creative as we wish. If you are anything like me and find hand stitching very difficult and slow, then you will really enjoy exploring your machine. Machine appliqué gives a consistent, perfect stitch every time.

The beautiful stitches on your machine will be used inside the flowers, leaves, clamshells, and vines, giving texture and decoration to the inner fused, raw edges. The visual focus then becomes the detail inside the flowers with different-colored threads and elaborate, decorative stitches. We will explore the use of thick threads and flat threads in different colors for impact while changing the settings of the stitches for maximum results.

Utilizing the Decorative Stitches on Your Machine

Have you tried pressing the buttons on your sewing machine to see which decorative stitches you have? I know it seems a little intimidating. Thoughts such as "What if I break my machine?" and "What if I do it all wrong?" might be going around in your mind. Let's try together to see what your machine can do. You never know what you will find. Machines have a Clear, or Reset, button. If you change the settings so much that you are confused, just hit Clear and the factory default setting will reset all width and lengths back to the start. You really cannot go wrong. Have fun getting to know your machine!

Most machines have at least a few decorative stitches. Some machines have hundreds of them. Generally, they are grouped together in themes, such as flowers, satin-based stitches, patchwork stitches, and cross-stitches.

The first group is usually the utility stitches, those we use often, such as straight stitch for piecing, zig-zag stitch, blind hem stitch and overlocking stitch. Groups of decorative stitches are usually in folders or in different modes. We will explore decorative stitches throughout this book. There are so many fun and exciting ways to use them, and I am thrilled to share them with you in these beautiful projects.

Stitching One Shape at a Time

Usually with raw-edge appliqué, the appliqué pieces are prepared and immediately pressed onto a background fabric to create the elements, such as flowers, leaves, and stems.

My technique is different. ⟶

In these projects, every flower is constructed separately by fusing its appliqué shapes together and pinning it to a very firm piece of stabilizer. The decorative stitching is then applied only to the inside areas and raw edges and never to the outside edge. This makes it so much easier to handle and turn the flower while applying the decorative stitches. If you make an error, simply throw away that flower and make another one without affecting the rest of your work. The number of different decorative stitches inside a flower is up to your imagination. Once you have stitched the inside, you will cut away the stabilizer and press the flower onto the background fabric. The outside raw edge is then free-motion sketch appliquéd.

Close-up of decorative stitches on inside edges
■ Photo by Deborah Louie

Why Sketch-Edge Appliqué for the Outer Edge?

You can choose to use a decorative stitch to cover the outside raw edge if you wish. However, you will need to do a great deal of turning and pushing of the whole project under the machine, particularly for a large quilt. It is annoying and inefficient, and really does not make good use of your time at the machine.

Sketch-edge appliqué is free-motion stitching that makes it easy to cover the raw edges. Working with the same color thread as the outside edge of the fabric and sketch-edge stitching one color at a time is so efficient and results in a beautiful, crisp edge. The focus is on the inside of the flower and your beautiful decorative stitching. I will be walking you through this process, so don't worry. It is so much fun!

Which Machine Feet to Use for Appliqué

For machine appliqué, you want maximum view of your needle and stitches. An open-toe embroidery foot or a clear appliqué foot is perfect. These feet have a small cutout groove underneath so they can glide over the stitches. They come standard with most machines. Different makes and models of machines have different stitch widths, such as 5.5mm, 7.0mm, or 9.0mm. To learn the width of your machine, move the width button or dial to the maximum setting. If your machine has a dual-feed function, this will help to evenly feed your appliqué shapes under the needle, and it will work well with stitching your decorative stitches.

Versions of open-toe embroidery feet for BERNINA machines
■ Photo by Deborah Louie

How to Set Up Your Machine

The information in this section is general, not machine-brand specific. For features that you are unsure about, please refer to your manual, contact your nearest dealer, or visit the website of your brand of sewing machine.

Foot pressure is important for the even feeding of stitches. In some machines, this is automatic, while on others it is a manual setting. Check your manual for the recommended standard foot pressure. If the pressure is too light, stitch length will be uneven. It if is too heavy, the fabric will buckle.

Some machines have auto foot lift. This means that when you have stopped stitching and the needle is down in your work, the foot will automatically lift and hover so that you can pivot or turn your fabric. A manual knee-operated lift achieves the same result. As you push against it with your right knee, the foot is lifted off the fabric. Both features are perfect for machine appliqué, making your stitching easier and more efficient and allowing you to keep your hands on your work.

Set your machine for "needle down" when the needle has stopped so that the needle stays in your stitching and will not move on to make the next stitch. This is important for excellent control.

 Hint: Use the knee lift with your right leg and foot pedal with your left foot. It takes only a little while to get used to it. You will enjoy hands-free, efficient stitching every time.

Understanding Your Sewing Machine's Features

Locate the width and length dials or buttons on your machine. Width makes any pattern wider or narrower. The length makes the stitches shorter or longer. Perhaps you have a needle-position dial or buttons. This changes the needle position to either the right or left of center. This is a wonderful feature to have.

Most machines have a mirror-reverse or turn-over key. This flips the design from left to right or up instead of down. There will be more on these when we are looking at side stitches.

Look for a "pattern begin" button. This symbol might be a triangle with a small line at the top. This restarts the pattern from the beginning. "Pattern end," which is a triangle with a line at the bottom, will finish the pattern. Some machines can be set to tie on at the beginning of pattern begin and tie off at the end of pattern end with approximately 4 stitches in one place, called *anchoring stitches*. There are brands of machines where this tie on is automatic when a new stitch is selected.

For consistent needle speed while you are stitching, set your speed dial or slide to slow or medium-slow speed and then press the foot pedal all the way to the floor. You can adjust the needle speed at any time for increased comfort. Slow stitching gives even-sized neat stitches every time.

How to Solve Machine Tension Problems

When it comes to the top tension dial on your machine, a lower number means a looser top thread, which results in more thread being delivered onto the fabric. If the tension is too low, the result will be loose stitching with loops on the back of the fabric, and the machine will often jam in the bobbin area.

#711 Tension

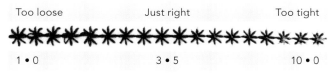

Too loose   Just right   Too tight

1 • 0   3 • 5   10 • 0

Tension problem from top

If the tension is too high, less thread is delivered onto the fabric, causing the top thread to pull the bobbin thread up to the front of the fabric. When this happens, the top thread often breaks. By changing the tension numbers a little at a time, you will achieve perfect tension. Remember, the higher the number, the higher the tension. To lower the tension, lower the number.

Back View

Too loose   Just right   Too tight

1 • 0   3 • 5   10 • 0

Tension problems from back

How to Tie On and Tie Off Stitching

To start machine appliqué stitching, we must ensure that the stitching will not unravel. We need to find out how your machine starts and stops. When stitching a new pattern, some machines will auto-matically start with the needle going up and down approximately 4 times in one spot; this is called *tying on*. On some machines, you can set this feature to occur automatically or press a knot button to activate it every time you need it. Similarly, for tying off at the end, you can set it or press a stop button, which is usually positioned just above the needle.

Before you start any of the projects, test both the starting tie-on and stopping tie-off features by selecting a decorative stitch, stitching it slowly, and observing what your machine does.

When to Use These Features

As we journey together through the many stitches in this book, I will teach you when and how to use these features to make your stitching enjoyable and efficient. You will be ready if you take time to familiarize yourself with these features at the beginning.

CHOOSING FABRIC COLORS

Solids Versus Prints for Maximum Impact

The use of solid-colored fabrics gives maximum stitch impact. You can clearly see and enjoy your decorative stitches and thread choices. The two samples of Ellen flower here demonstrate this well by comparing the use of solid-colored fabrics with colored print fabrics.

Comparing solids with prints on Ellen

The use of busy prints hides the beautiful decorative stitches, which is a shame. Prints also take away from the individual shapes of Ellen because the eye does not know where to sit and enjoy the beauty of the flower.

Solids come in a huge variety of colors from most fabric manufacturers. For these projects, shopping for one color at a time in many different values is perfect. The *value* of a color is the lightness to darkness of the color. For example, imagine pink from the lightest pastel pink to baby pink, lolly pink, and hot pink. One color but many values. The word *chroma* describes how clean or dirty a color is and, when a color is a little dirty or grayed, it draws attention to a bright, clean color nearby. I have used a few of these grayed chromas, like plum and steel blue, in my projects.

I call solids my "pantry fabrics." These are the fabrics that I keep in good quantities and use for many different quilts. They are stored in drawers labelled by their color—for example, there is a drawer for solid yellows, a drawer for solid oranges, and so on. When the fabrics in a drawer are running low, I go and have some fun shopping at my favorite quilt shops. I always cut a small amount of fabric that I want to replace or add to a project, paste it onto some paper or a notebook, and use it to check that I am purchasing the perfect missing color.

> I call a print that is very strong and memorable my "hero fabric," and I usually use it in one quilt only.

Choosing a Color Palette for the Projects

For the projects in this book, I have used only solids in clean, bright colors that are mostly on the warm side of the color wheel. I chose pinks, reds, purples, oranges, and yellows, all in a number of gradation values. I aimed for a lovely, soft transition from yellow to orange to coral to pink.

Then, to add pop or excitement to the work, I chose some cool complementary colors, such as blues, green/blues, limes, and yellow/greens, which are found on the opposite side of the color wheel from the warm colors.

The addition of black fabric and thread brings the large range of colors together nicely and highlights them all.

The projects include neutral backgrounds like grays, whites, and ombré blues so that the composition of the flowers is the hero, not a printed background fabric. Additionally, the background free-motion quilting stands out so nicely on solids.

Please use your own color preferences and be as creative as you like. For example, if you are making the runner for your home, you may want to look at the color decor of your home and include those colors in your runner.

Color palettes for the four projects

Balancing Colors Across Your Project

The first decision to make in choosing colors for the flowers is whether they will be predominately bright, with a mixture of warm and cool colors, or only one or two colors in various values.

With the Little Garden Cushion (page 104), I chose purple, turquoise, pink, and orange. I drew up a quick sketch of the project on some sketching paper using the patterns in this book. As I made the flowers, I pinned them onto the drawing on my design wall. This really helped me to get a nice balance and distribution of the colors throughout the project.

Next, I added the smaller flowers and leaves and, finally, the clamshell border, bringing all of the colors harmoniously together.

I would recommend that you try this step-by-step process of color choice, concentrating on one flower at a time. Try to think about the shapes inside a flower. If they are all the same color value, the individual units of the flower will disappear. Try to use colors that contrast, such as a light-colored outside shape with a dark-colored shape on top. This will create a strong, vibrant appliqué story for your cushion or runner.

Color palette layout for Little Garden Cushion

To Wash or Not to Wash?

Well, isn't that the question? It is entirely your personal preference to prewash and press your fabrics before using them in a project. Personally, I don't because I prefer the feel of unwashed fabric, which is firm and crisp, and the thought of pressing yards and yards of fabric that have been washed is exhausting.

When washing the finished project, I put a few dye-catching sheets into the washing machine. Any excess dye that leaves the fabric will be absorbed by these amazing sheets, which can be found in the laundry section of most supermarkets.

Hint: If you are giving your project to someone as a gift, it is a good idea to include some dye-catching sheets with it.

Which Needles to Use

There is a huge variety of sewing machine needles to choose from, and it can be confusing. To choose, look at both needle size and type.

The size of the needle, such as 100/16, 90/14, 80/12, and 70/10, indicates its thickness. The higher the number, the thicker the needle. I always use a size 90 or 100 needle when machine appliquéing through multiple layers of fused fabrics and stabilizer. A size 100 needle makes a large hole that is perfect for thick thread such as 12-weight cotton. Using a finer or smaller needle results in skipped stitches.

Consider the type of needle next. There are quite a few types of needles—quilting, topstitch, denim, universal, metallic, and stretch. Confused?

For appliqué and decorative stitching, I always use size 90 or 100 topstitch needle. Topstitch needles are perfect because they have a very large eye, which prevents the threads from heating up and breaking. When threaded with 12-weight threads, topstitch needles stitch beautifully.

Size 80 quilting needles stitch well for machine quilting. However, if I have a lot of ditch stitching in the appliqué, then I switch to a size 90 topstitch needle. This needle does a better job of piercing through the thickness of the appliqué shapes and decorative stitching.

If you get a few skipped stitches, change to a new needle—your needle is most likely blunt.

Self-Threading Needles

Self-threading hand-stitching needles are always by my machine for pulling the ends of threads to the back of my work and then knotting and cutting them. This is a lovely, neat way to finish stitching. The needles have an opening at the top to pop the thread into for quick threading. They are available from many quilt shops.

Differences in Threads

Just like needles, the range of threads is enormous. The thicker the thread, the lower the number on the cone. For example, size 12 is a thick thread and size 100 is very fine. Yes, thread size is opposite to needle size! Again, confusing. Size 100 is a fine thread and, if it is used for appliquéing, it is hardly noticeable.

Collection of threads and needles

Throughout this book, I have used a few different types and sizes of threads. No thread is out of bounds when appliquéing, but I do have favorites.

• Cotton threads are round and sit up off the fabric. When they are used for a decorative open stitch, the pattern looks three-dimensional. A 12-weight cotton thread is thicker than a 50-weight cotton thread, and so it produces a thicker stitch pattern. Aurifil, Gütermann, and WonderFil's Spagetti lines all have beautiful 12-weight cotton threads.

• Shiny, 40-weight 100% polyester threads are flat (they are called trilobal three-sided threads), which makes them perfect for shiny satin-based stitches, where the stitches sit closely together. Using shiny polyester thread produces dense, flat stitch patterns that the machine's appliqué foot glides over smoothly. Look for the shiny polyester threads; not all polyester threads are flat, but shiny polyesters are becoming more readily available. I use shiny polyester threads for all my free-motion quilting as well. Some examples are Mettler's POLY SHEEN, WonderFil's Polyfast, and Gem threads.

For years, embroiderers have used rayon threads, but I find they are soft and break easily. And since I use shiny polyester for quilting as well as appliqué, I find it makes more economic sense to invest in shiny polyester instead of two ranges of threads.

50-weight cotton

40-weight polyester

12-weight cotton

Different threads give the same stitch different effects.

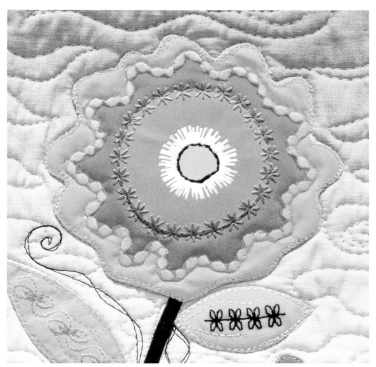

Close-up of Jenny from Little Garden Cushion, with different weights of threads

Hint: If a thread is delivered straight off the cone, stand it up straight on the vertical spool holder. If a thread is cross wound (I call this "crissy-crossy"), place the cone horizontally on the horizontal spool holder.

Using Specialty Threads

When machine quilting, I like to use clear MonoPoly thread (by Superior Threads) to ditch quilt most of my quilts, whether pieced or appliquéd. This clear polyester thread is flexible, absorbs the color of the fabric, and makes the appliqué sit beautifully on the surface of the work. And since it is polyester, it can be pressed with an iron, unlike nylon thread, which cannot be pressed.

Rayon threads are known for their luster and are lovely in appliqué, but they are soft and tend to break easily. If you use them, stitch slowly with reduced top tension (smaller number).

Metallic threads add some magic to any quilt. Purchase the best quality thread you can. Use a metallic or top-stitch needle, stitch slowly, and reduce top tension for best results.

Why Use Bobbin Fill Thread?

Bobbin fill thread is a very fine 100% polyester used for machine embroidery. This thread is inexpensive, strong, and fine. It usually comes in black and white. For black or very dark top threads, use black bobbin fill thread. For all light and bright colors, use white. Bobbin fill thread will not bulk up the stitching, and the embroidery foot can smoothly travel over the stitching. It is available in many quilt shops.

As this thread is very fine, I use a special tighter yellow bobbin case in my BERNINA 770 QE machine when I stitch with this finer thread, and I rarely need to change the top tension. Check with your local machine dealer to see if your machine has an option for a tighter bobbin case.

If the bobbin fill thread comes to the top of the work as you stitch, reduce your top thread tension a little. If this does not solve the problem, tighten the bobbin case if you are comfortable doing so. The rule here is turn the tension screw right to tighten and left to loosen.

Choosing a Color Palette of Threads

As with a fabric color palette, you need a bright, colorful thread color palette.

For sketch-edge appliqué on an outside edge, use colored 100% polyester flat thread that matches the fabric edge color as closely as possible. If you have a large variety of fabric colors, each color will need a matching colored thread.

Using 12-weight cotton threads in colors from your fabric palette will enhance and add texture to your stitching. I recommend adding black and white to your 12-weight cotton thread palette. Black will catch the eye and draw out a shape or area in the appliqué. White will give a lovely fresh effect to any area of the appliqué. Additionally, black and white draw attention to the bright colors in your palette.

Add some specialty threads like metallic silver or gold for that little bit of glamour and to draw attention to your favorite flower.

Stabilizer

While stitching, you must use stabilizer behind each appliqué shape. After stitching, cut away the excess but leave in the stabilizer behind the decorative stitching. I use a dressmaking grade of heavyweight, nonwoven stabilizer, equal to that in a shirt with a stiff, firm collar. My favorite is Vilene. If the stabilizer is too soft, the machine stitching will buckle and the flowers will pull in and distort. Do not use a fusible stabilizer; they are difficult to remove.

Fusible Webbing

Double-sided paper-backed fusible webbing is produced by many manufacturers and is known by many brand names. Look for fusible webbing that is lightly glued. My favorite is Vliesofix Bondaweb (by Vlieseline), a very lightly glued product. Please do not use the tacky-to-the-touch webbings, as the glue is too thick and causes fraying of the raw edges during edge stitching. Baking or parchment paper is also helpful when pressing the fusible webbing.

Temporary Glue

When basting the quilts, I suggest temporary spray adhesive. I use Odif 505 Temporary Fabric Adhesive spray. I also use temporary washable glue for areas that may need a bit more gluing. I use Roxanne Glue-Baste-It.

Appliqué Pressing Sheet

My method requires a see-through nonstick mat, sometimes called an appliqué pressing sheet. The sheet protects your ironing surface and makes creating the layered flowers so easy.

Batting

The perfect batting is a medium-loft 100% polyester batting with scrim. Scrimmed batting has a fine base of nonwoven interfacing that has been glued or needle-punched into the batting. The scrim stops the fibers from drifting apart and separating, and makes the batting strong and very durable.

PREPARING

APPLIQUÉ SHAPES

FOR STITCHING

FLOWER CONSTRUCTION BASICS

Stacking Flowers or Layering Flowers

I named my collection of flowers and leaves after members of my family and close friends. Just like us, each has their own personality and uniqueness. Each flower has been designed and hand drawn by me. Some of the flowers are very symmetrical and perfect looking, while others are asymmetrical and, let's say, a little quirky.

For the purpose of constructing the flowers, I have placed them in two categories.

- **Stacked shapes:** Stacked shapes are fused one by one on top of each other, starting with the largest shape at the bottom (shape 1) and continuing in numerical order to the last shape on the top.

- **Layered shapes:** Layered shapes are built up from the pattern sheet, fusing them one at a time, starting from shape 1 and working in numerical order to the last shape.

Stacking technique for Doreen (*left*) and layering technique for Eileen (*right*)

Flowers

STACKED FLOWERS

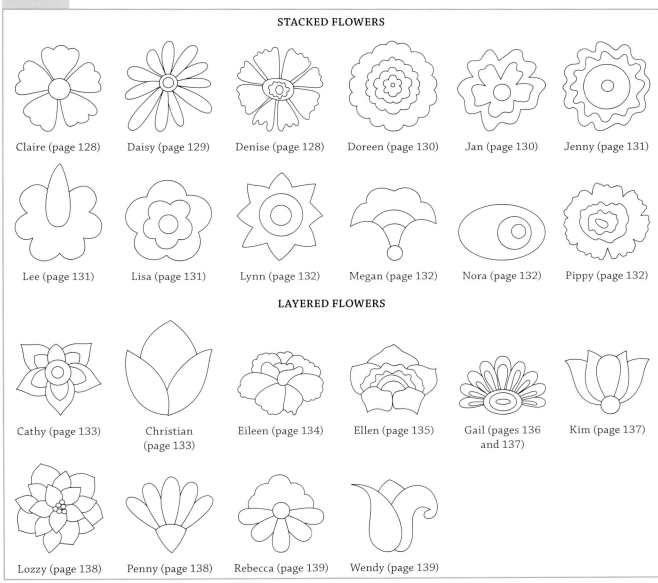

Claire (page 128)

Daisy (page 129)

Denise (page 128)

Doreen (page 130)

Jan (page 130)

Jenny (page 131)

Lee (page 131)

Lisa (page 131)

Lynn (page 132)

Megan (page 132)

Nora (page 132)

Pippy (page 132)

LAYERED FLOWERS

Cathy (page 133)

Christian (page 133)

Eileen (page 134)

Ellen (page 135)

Gail (pages 136 and 137)

Kim (page 137)

Lozzy (page 138)

Penny (page 138)

Rebecca (page 139)

Wendy (page 139)

Leaves (page 140)

SYMMETRICAL LEAVES

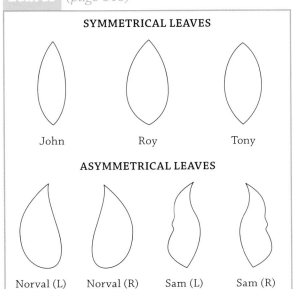

John

Roy

Tony

ASYMMETRICAL LEAVES

Norval (L)

Norval (R)

Sam (L)

Sam (R)

Clamshells (page 141)

4˝ full clamshell

3˝ full clamshell

3˝ border clamshell

Symmetrical and Asymmetrical Designs

Raw-edge appliqué uses fusible webbing to adhere the fabric shapes to each other and the base fabric. The shapes must first be divided into single individual units drawn on fusible webbing. How this is done depends on whether the design is symmetrical or asymmetrical.

Look at each flower or leaf to see if it is symmetrical or asymmetrical. For example, compare the two flowers Doreen and Eileen in the illustration below. Doreen is the flower on the left. When a line is drawn through the center of Doreen, both sides are the same. This flower is symmetrical. When a line is drawn through Eileen, the flower on the right, both sides are different. This flower is asymmetrical.

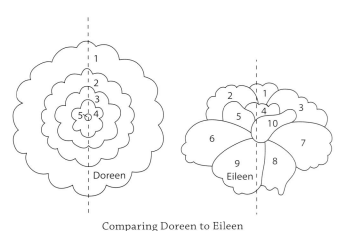

Comparing Doreen to Eileen

How to Prepare Designs for Fusing

Symmetrical Shapes

Because Doreen is symmetrical, you can draw its shapes on the fusible webbing exactly as they are in the flower pattern. Press each shape onto the wrong side of the fabric, cut it out, flip it over, and press with the fabric right side up to make the flower.

Doreen's shapes are placed straight on top of each other from largest to smallest using the stacking technique. The shapes are numbered from 1 to 5 in the order of their size, shape 1 being the largest shape and shape 5 being the tiny center circle.

Asymmetrical Shapes

Because Eileen is an asymmetrical flower, its shapes must be mirror reversed for drawing. To do this, turn the pattern over and trace the reversed pattern on the fusible webbing. Press each shape onto the wrong side of the fabric, cut it out, flip it over, and press with the fabric right side up to make the flower.

Eileen is constructed using the layering technique. The shapes are numbered from 1 to 10 in the order that they are used to make the flower. Place shape 1 first at the base and end with shape 10 at the top. The dotted lines on the pattern mean that this part of the shape will be overlapped by another shape. I added ⅛″ to each overlapped shape along the dotted lines to allow for the overlap.

On the pattern pages (pages 127–142), the shapes are numbered and reversed for you. Each flower and leaf is true to size for the projects, so you do not have to enlarge any shapes.

You simply trace, press, cut, and stitch!

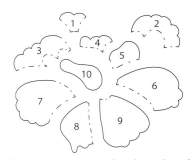

Eileen pieces reversed and numbered

Clamshell Borders

The clamshell borders come in 2 different sizes for the Little Garden Cushion and the Garden Runner. For the cushion, the 4″ (10.2cm) clamshell shape has a small arch in the center. The runner uses a 3″ (7.6cm) clamshell. A few of the 3″ (7.6cm) clamshells are fully shaped, but most have a flat edge at the bottom, which makes them sit very nicely on the outer edge of the runner. Because the clamshell shape is symmetrical, reversing of the shapes is not necessary.

Close-up of Little Garden Cushion's clamshell border

PREPARING FUSIBLE SHAPES

Drawing the Pattern Pieces

Double-sided paper-backed fusible webbing is produced by many manufacturers and is known by many brand names. Fusible paper has a smooth side, which we trace the shapes onto with a pencil, and a rough side, which holds the glue. My favorite is Vliesofix Bondaweb because it is a very lightly glued product. Please do not use the tacky-to-the-touch webbings as the glue is too thick and fraying of the raw edges is common.

Hint: *If the glue on the fusible paper is too thick, the fused shape sits a bit above the background during the final construction. This slight distance can cause fraying when you edge-stitch appliqué the shape to the background later in the process.*

Place the fusible paper over the top of the pattern. Trace every individual shape, leaving a ½″ (1.3cm) gap between each one. Label each with the pattern name and piece number. Using small scissors, cut out the fusible paper shapes ¼″ (0.6cm) outside the drawn line. Place the pieces for each flower in a resealable airtight

bag to protect the fusible from drying out and to keep all the pieces together.

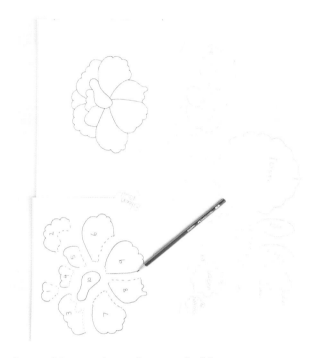

Eileen and Doreen shapes drawn on fusible paper

Pressing the Pieces to the Fabric

Use a hot iron to press each shape onto the wrong side of its fabric. If you are using solid fabric, then there is no right or wrong side. Turn the fabric over and press the other side to ensure that the glue is firmly attached to the fabric.

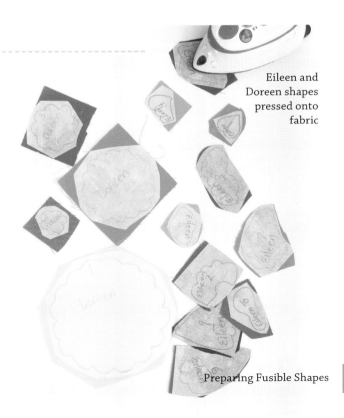

Eileen and Doreen shapes pressed onto fabric

Cutting Out the Pieces

Once each pressed fabric shape has cooled, use a small, sharp pair of scissors to cut out the shape exactly on the drawn line. Place it back into its bag.

Eileen and Doreen shapes pressed and cut out

Clamshells

The Little Garden Cushion has a 4″ (10.2cm) clamshell with separate arch. The Garden Runner has a 3″ (7.6cm) single clamshell with a marked arch to stitch that can be used full-size or with a flat bottom for border treatments.

1. Place the fusible paper over the top of the clamshell pattern for the project you have selected.

2. Trace each individual shape, leaving a ½″ (1.3cm) gap between all the shapes. Using small scissors, cut each of the shapes ¼″ (0.6cm) outside the drawn line. Place the pieces in a resealable plastic bag.

3. Follow the instructions for Pressing the Pieces to the Fabric (page 21) and Cutting Out the Pieces (page 22) to finish preparing the clamshell fusibles.

 Hint: For large quantities of clamshells, as in the runner, use template plastic to make your own templates for the clamshell shapes.

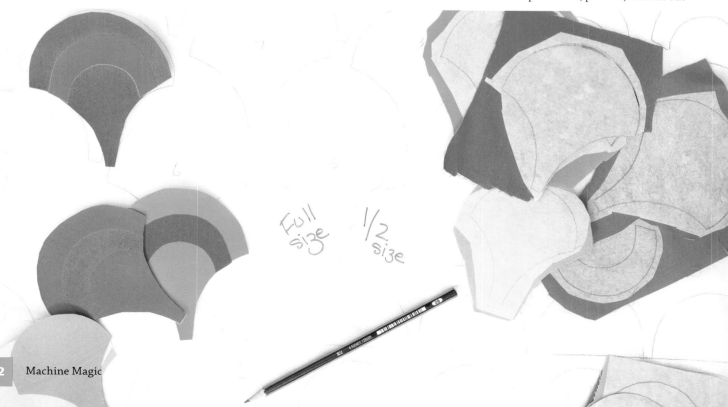

Clamshell shapes drawn, pressed, and cut out

BUILDING THE APPLIQUÉ SHAPES

Stacked and Layered Flowers

All the flowers in this book fall into one of two categories according to their construction technique: either stacking or layering (see Meet the Members of the Garden Family, page 19).

In the following examples, I have used Doreen to demonstrate the stacking technique and Eileen to demonstrate the layering technique. To construct your flowers, follow the same step-by-step processes. It becomes easy with practice!

If you are very new to decorative machine stitching, it's a good idea to make a few extra flowers, leaves, and clamshells just in case you are not completely happy with your first round of stitching. If you don't need them, you have some bonus flowers to use for a quilt label or another small project. It's good to be prepared for your next project.

Stacking Technique

We are using Doreen (page 130) to demonstrate the stacking technique.

1. Keep the composite drawing for Doreen in front of you. The composite drawings are on the same page as the pattern pieces for the stacked flowers.

2. With a pin, score the edge of shape 1 to easily fold back and remove the fusible backing paper.

3. Referring to the composite drawing, place the shape 1, fusible side down, on the appliqué mat in its position on the pattern sheet. Lightly press with a hot iron.

4. Score and remove the paper from the remaining shapes.

5. Place the shapes one by one in numerical order on top of each other, making sure to center them, and press.

6. Cut a 6″ × 6″ (15.2 × 15.2cm) square of heavyweight stabilizer. Pin the square behind Doreen.

Doreen completed with stabilizer

Layering Technique

We are using Eileen (page 134) to demonstrate the layering technique.

1. Trace or copy the composite drawing of Eileen and place it under the appliqué mat.

2. Using a pin, score the edge of shape 1 and remove the paper.

3. Place the shape 1, fusible side down, on the appliqué mat in its place on the composite drawing. Lightly press with a hot iron.

4. Remove the paper from shape 2 and put it into position on the pattern sheet, with an ⅛″ (0.3cm) overlap over the top of the first shape. Press.

5. Remove the paper from shape 3 and put it into position. Press.

Eileen

1

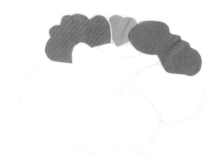

2

3

6. Continue to place the remaining shapes in numerical order.

4

5

6

7   8   9

Shape 10 completes the flower.

10

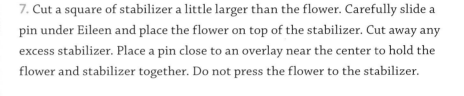

7. Cut a square of stabilizer a little larger than the flower. Carefully slide a pin under Eileen and place the flower on top of the stabilizer. Cut away any excess stabilizer. Place a pin close to an overlay near the center to hold the flower and stabilizer together. Do not press the flower to the stabilizer.

Eileen completed with stabilizer

Pressing Clamshells Using the Stacking Technique

This method applies to the 4˝ (10.2cm) clamshell used in the Little Garden Cushion.

1. Using a pin, score the edge of the small arch shape and remove the paper. Leave the paper on the clamshell shape.

2. Place each arch on top of the clamshell and press.

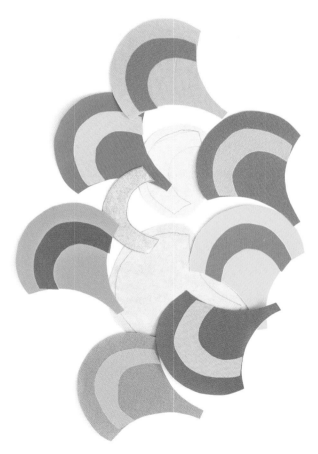

Clamshells being prepared for stitching

3. Cut a small strip of stabilizer to place behind the small arch of the 4˝ (10.2cm) clamshell and the top of each 3˝ (7.6cm) clamshell to support the stitching.

Why Use Stabilizer?

You must use stabilizer behind each appliqué shape. Without a stabilizer behind the shapes, the machine stitching will draw in and pucker them, possibly causing your machine to jam with thread and your work to fall apart, making a big mess.

Eileen, Jenny, Penny, and Ellen pinned on stabilizer

The stabilizer I use is a dressmaking grade of heavy-weight, nonwoven Vilene. This is very inexpensive and should be available in most quilt shops or haberdashery stores.

Try a few grades first to see which one really supports your stitching. If the stabilizer is too light, your appliqué will not sit flat. You will remove most of the stabilizer after you have completed the decorative stitching, but you will leave the stabilizer behind the stitching itself to continue to support it.

I like to pin the prepared leaves on one large piece of stabilizer, grouping them together in their individual shapes. It is easy to stitch, and the tiny leaves are not misplaced.

DECORATIVE STITCHING, ONE SHAPE AT A TIME

UNDERSTANDING PERFECT STITCH-PATTERN PLACEMENT

Finding the Rhythm of a Stitch Pattern

I know this heading might sound a little strange, but it is necessary to learn the rhythm of each stitch pattern—how the decorative stitch is formed and when the stitch pattern finishes before it stitches into the next repeat of the pattern. This is very important for precise, neat embroidery stitching that you will be thrilled with.

Let's look at the star pattern on my BERNINA 770 QE, stitch number 711. It is a centerline pattern, which means that the pattern sits on both sides of the centerline. It starts at the top (12 o'clock) and then travels left and right, coming back into the center every time.

The very last section of the stitch to complete the pattern formation finishes at the bottom of the star (6 o'clock).

When the star is finished, a new star starts again at the top (12 o'clock). While this is a common stitch on many machines, different brands of machines will have a different stitch sequence. Test your stitches to get to know the stitch pattern well. This will help you feel so much more comfortable and confident.

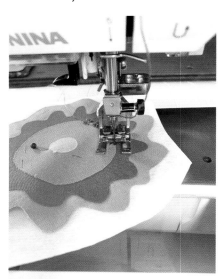

■ Photo by Deborah Louie

■ Photo by Deborah Louie

Needle stopped down and ready to start a new star

■ Photo by Deborah Louie

To find this rhythm, stitch very slowly on your test fabric.

- Watch how the pattern is formed and where to stop the needle before it travels onto the beginning of the next star.

- Check your machine for a pattern repeat button; this is where you can set how many repeats you wish to stitch. Set the repeat for only 1 repeat. The machine will stop with the needle down at the finish position. Alternatively, when you start stitching, press the end or finish button to stop after 1 repeat of any design.

Hint: *If your flower or test fabric buckles or does not lie flat, use a firmer heavyweight stabilizer rather than doubling up a midweight one.*

Positioning of the Embroidery Foot

The position of the embroidery foot is very important for neat, perfect stitching. If the decorative stitch is a centerline pattern, the raw edge of the shape must be in the center of the embroidery foot.

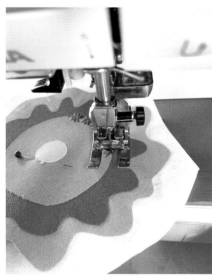

◼ Photo by Deborah Louie

With a side-line pattern, the inside edge of the foot must be just a fraction off the raw edge of the shape. If the raw edge is *not* parallel or running in the same angle to the inside of the presser foot, then your next decorative stitch will not cover the raw edge.

Raw edge to the left of the inside of the embroidery foot

◼ Photo by Deborah Louie

Perfecting Corners and Points

Once you have learned the formation, rhythm, and placement of the stitch pattern, you can look at stitching the perfect corners or points.

For the star pattern, the needle stops in the center after each pattern repeat except for the final repeat, which finishes the star pattern at 6 o'clock.

Needle stopped in center position of star

◼ Photo by Deborah Louie

1. To turn a corner while stitching this pattern, stop the needle in the center of the star, lift the presser foot, and pivot the fabric so that the final stitch of the star will sit on the raw edge. Stitch this final stitch and stop.

2. Pivot the fabric again, if necessary, so that the next raw edge will sit perfectly parallel to the inside of the embroidery foot.

To practice this precise stitching, I suggest setting your machine to a slow speed with the needle always stopping in the down position. Draw a line or shape and stitch this a few times on practice fabric until you are happy with your stitch placement.

Stitching last stitch of star at point

■ Photo by Deborah Louie

Star finished and ready to start a new star with edge parallel

■ Photo by Deborah Louie

The line / raw edge is not parallel to the embroidery foot.

■ Photo by Deborah Louie

When to Pivot

It is very important to allow the machine to sew one stitch at a time, stop with your needle down in your work, and then pivot or turn your work. Pivoting or turning while the stitch is being formed will result in very distorted decorative stitches.

• On Leaf A, the length of the star was too long and the corner did not work out well.

• Leaf B was stitched inside the line and outside the line, which would leave the raw edge uncovered.

• On Leaf C, pivoting was done while stitching the center of the stars, which made the stitching distorted and not form well.

• Leaf D is well stitched. At both the top and bottom points, the last stitch was made slightly longer to meet the point exactly and the needle was stopped before the fabric was pivoted.

Stars stitched on leaf shapes A to D

Hint: Before you start, prepare many sets of fabric and stabilizer for testing your stitches, tension, and number of repeats needed.

LEARNING THE STITCHES ON YOUR MACHINE

Making a Stitch Diary

I always ask my students to keep a stitch diary in which they stitch and record all the decorative stitches on their machines. I encourage you to do this before venturing onto one of these projects. Though it may take a while to do if you have many decorative stitches on your machine, you will have an amazing record of what your machine can do, and you will learn a great deal about your machine.

1. Purchase a plastic pocket display folder and cut white or light-colored fabric and heavyweight stabilizer to fit the folder.

2. Choose the first stitch. On the fabric where the stitching will begin, write the default setting, which is the stitch length and width preset by the machine.

3. Stitch this for a few inches, then change the length and widths and record your settings as you travel down the fabric. Perhaps draw a straight line to follow.

4. Repeat for each stitch on your machine.

I am always excited to do this whenever I purchase a new machine. Different brands and models of sewing machines have varying stitches. So if you're an owner of multiple machines, why not make a diary for each machine? I have been known to have three machines on my table at one time, all set up doing different stitches.

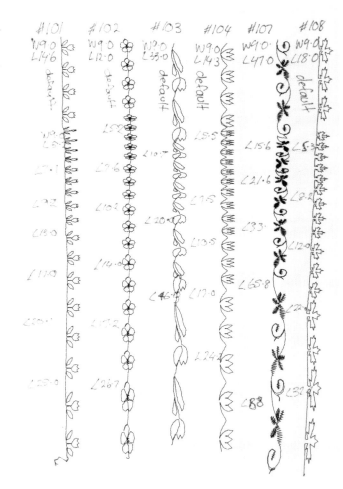

Page from a stitch diary folder

Hint: For best results when decorative stitching, stitch slowly. Stitching too fast can unbalance some stitches.

The Very Useful Triple Stitch

The triple stitch is a straight stitch that travels forward, back, and forward again. You should find this in your utility stitches on the front of your machine or in the first folder. On my BERNINA 770 QE, it is 6. This is such a versatile stitch.

Using a 12-weight thread, a size 90 topstitch needle, and bobbin fill thread in the bobbin, test this stitch on a trial piece of fabric with a heavyweight stabilizer underneath. Change the length gradually and record the number right up to the maximum length. Triple stitches get more dramatic the longer they are. With the 12-weight thread, you get more impact because it is thicker than a 50-weight thread. Try both 12-weight and 50-weight threads with the same length setting to see the difference. Remember to stitch slowly.

This stitch is so valuable because if a decorative stitch does not cover the raw edge sufficiently, simply go back over the edge with a triple stitch and it will be covered nicely in the same thread or a contrast color for extra zing.

There are many uses of triple stitch in these projects. The small Tony leaves have black triple stitch in the center. On Claire's petals, the light blue triple stitches highlight the pretty decorative stitch between them. On Lynn, the butterfly stitch around the larger purple circle had only a single stitch along the center, which was not enough to cover the raw edge, so I came back and triple stitched over it. I also added a pop of orange 12-weight thread with triple stitch on the raw edge of the smaller blue circle.

Claire with triple stitch inside petals

Lynn and a Tony leaf with triple stitches added

Triple and chain stitch sample

Chain Straight Stitch

Do you have an even heavier straight stitch on your machine? On my BERNINA 770 QE, I have a straight stitch which travels back and forward 7 times, stitch pattern 713. This stitch used with a 12-weight cotton thread looks just like hand-sewn chain stitching. It is so effective! I have used it in black 12-weight cotton thread to stitch the vines connecting the flowers on Little Garden Cushion. It is wonderful to use if you want more of a visual impact.

Close-up detail of chain-stitched vines in black thread

CENTERLINE DECORATIVE STITCHES

These stitches have a straight line down the middle of the pattern, and the decorative stitch travels left and right of this line. As you stitch, place the straight line on the raw edge of the appliqué shape. For example, look at the blue 12-weight thread stitching the star pattern here on Jenny. The centerline of the star covers the raw edge perfectly.

Star Stitch and Adjusting for Variety

Let's look at this star pattern more closely.

When you turn the machine on and select this star or something similar (on my BERNINA 770 QE it is stitch 711), the default setting is 9.0 for the width (which is the maximum width) and 7.9 for the length. The default setting is sometimes known as the *preset setting.*

By adjusting the length and width dials, you can get so many different looks for this one pattern. Changing to maximum length elongates the star, and reducing the length brings the stars closer together, making the star stitch look like a completely different pattern.

What we are doing here and throughout this book is not only using the default settings but also having fun changing the settings to get an unlimited number of different looks from the decorative stitches that are available on your sewing machine.

Centerline star stitch and satin ball stitch on raw edge of Jenny
■ Photo by Deborah Louie

Testing for Accurate Pattern Repeats

The stitch length is where the fine adjustment occurs for achieving the perfect number of pattern repeats. Take, for example, the center circle from Jenny. Using a constant width of 9.0, I tested the default length of 11.9 but ended up with either a gap or an overlap, which were not nice looks at all. By changing the length to 9.0, I got a perfect meeting point. Testing your settings first really is worth the time for accurate, beautiful decorative stitching. You may need to make a few attempts to get the perfect stitch adjustment. Be patient; test every stitch before applying it to your flowers.

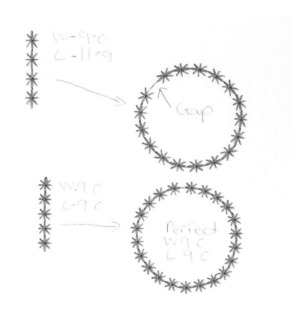

Testing Jenny's circle by adjusting length

Star pattern with changed settings from my stitch diary

Look at Daisy. I have used only star stitch 711 on this flower, and I am thrilled with the different effects I have achieved. One stitch in different lengths and widths results in so many looks. Fabulous, isn't it, to have so much fun exploring your sewing machine?

Daisy shows many ways to adjust one decorative stitch.

Discovering More Centerline Stitches

There may be more centerline stitches on your machine, like the ones here that I have stitched out. Can you see that I have had fun changing the width and length? Always write down your changes on your fabric and add them into your stitch diary.

If the center line of stitching on a centerline pattern is only single stitches and too light, stitch over these center stitches again with a triple stitch in the same color. Or perhaps try a thread of a different color or size for variety.

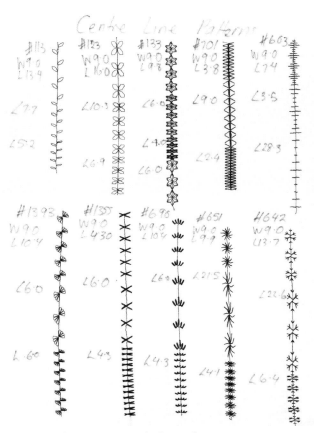

More centerline patterns with changed settings

Lynn, with an extra line of stitching over the centerline pattern
■ Photo by Deborah Louie

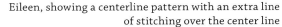

Eileen, showing a centerline pattern with an extra line
of stitching over the center line

SIDE-LINE DECORATIVE STITCHES

These stitches have a straight line along the side of the pattern.

Side-line triangle stitching

■ Photo by Deborah Louie

They work very well on the raw edge facing outward, mostly better than inward. You can explore your machine's side-line stitches by changing the width and length to make new patterns. If the stitches along the side line have not completely covered the raw edge, go back over the original stitching with a triple stitch (page 32).

If your machine has a mirror-reverse button, you can use it to flip the design from sitting on the right-hand side to the left-hand side and vice versa. On my BERNINA 770 QE, the mirror-reverse icon is two triangles—one solid and one outline only. On some machines, this might be called a *TOM (turn over motor) button*. If you have a mirror-reverse up-and-down button, then the stitch patterns can travel up or down.

Work through your stitch diary with your side-line stitches, adjusting the width and length to create many more stitches to use on your projects.

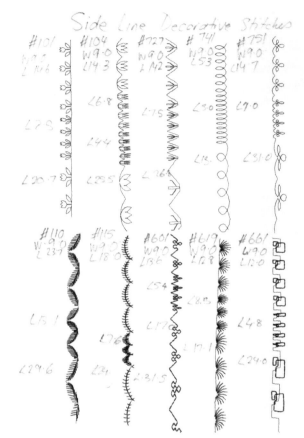

Some side-line patterns stitched out in my stitch diary

Unless you practice the different patterns using varying lengths and widths, you have no idea how pretty they can look on your appliqué. Side-line patterns work very well facing outward. And a triple stitch in a contrasting thread adds to the colorful play of the appliqué.

Detail of side-line stitches on Gail

THE WONDERFUL BLANKET STITCH

The Difference in Blanket Stitches

The blanket stitch is one of my favorite types of stitches and is really a go-to stitch when I am appliquéing. I often say, "Thank goodness for my machine," as my hand stitching is so awful. I have no idea how to hand stitch blanket stitching, and I don't need to learn when my machine can stitch it beautifully for me.

There are three main styles of blanket stitching—light, medium, and heavy. The trick to getting a perfect result is to count the stitches. Take your next testing piece and stitch out the blanket-stitch options on your machine to get to know them. Please note where the stitch starts. Does it start with a horizontal stitch first or a vertical stitch? This is important to know.

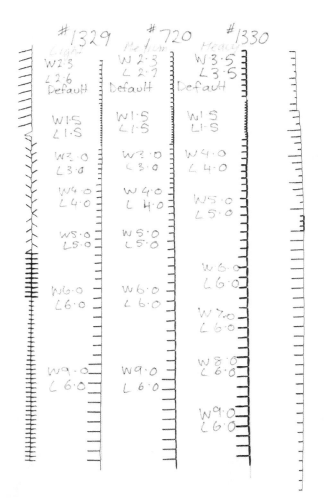

Blanket stitch diary entry

Single Blanket Stitch

The single blanket stitch follows a sequence of 1 stitch down (vertical) and 2 stitches across (horizontal). I count this as a 1–2 combination. Only one stitch covers the raw edge, which can be difficult because it often misses the raw edge. However, it has a lovely, delicate, light stitch look, particularly when the thread color is the same as the color of the fabric. It produces a barely there look.

Medium Blanket Stitch

Medium blanket stitch follows a sequence of 3 stitches down (vertical) and 2 stitches across (horizontal). I count this as a 3–2 combination. You have 3 stitches now to cover the raw edge and 2 stitches across. This is my favorite for blanket stitching traditional appliqué. This stitch formation will be found on most brands and models of machines.

Heavy Blanket Stitch

Heavy blanket stitch follows a sequence of 5 stitches down (vertical) and 4 stitches across (horizontal). I count this as a 5–4 combination. This many stitches covering the raw edge makes the appliqué very durable. It gives an amazing look when using 12-weight cotton thread, which is already thick, and selecting a large length and width. It looks just like hand stitching but so much better than my hand stitching ever could be. Take your stitching slowly to really count the stitches for accuracy when pivoting.

Single Blanket Stitch

1 stitch down (vertical) and 2 stitches across (horizontal)

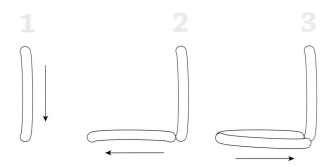

Medium Blanket Stitch

3 stitches down (vertical) and 2 stitches across (horizontal)

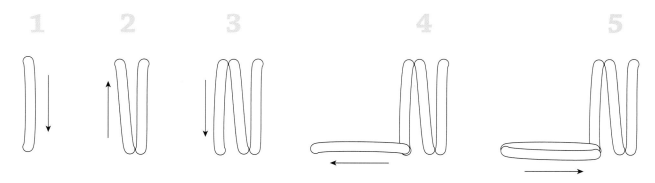

Heavy Blanket Stitch

5 stitches down (vertical) and 4 stitches across (horizontal)

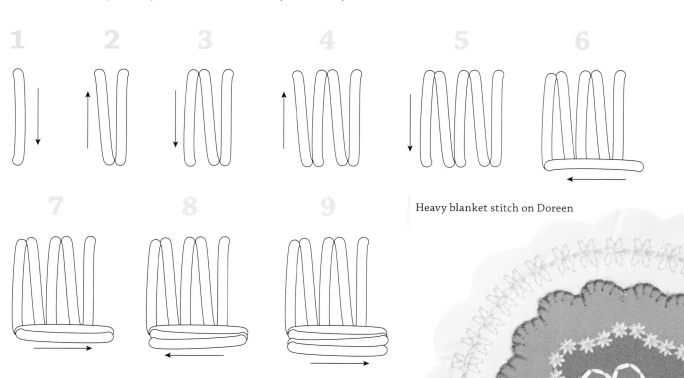

Heavy blanket stitch on Doreen

Adjusting Width, Length, and Needle Position

Use your width and length dials or buttons to adjust the blanket stitches for variety. You will find some fun variations.

When you use the width dial to make your stitch narrower, the needle position travels more toward the center. This is easy to fix if you have a needle-position button like my BERNINA 770 QE sewing machine. If you do have it, move the needle position either all the way to the left or all the way to the right, depending on which side you have your straight edge. This way your raw edge is right up against the side edge of the embroidery foot. This is a simple trick, but it is extremely handy for precise stitching. Unfortunately, this feature is not on all brands of machines.

Long medium blanket stitch on Cathy from Garden Runner

It is so exciting to see the blanket stitches when they are taken off the default setting. I enjoy using a short length with maximum width. With a 12-weight thread, the stitch looks like eyelashes.

Counting the Stitches

For beautiful blanket stitching, align the side of your open-toe embroidery foot with the edge of the fabric. If you keep the side of the foot parallel with the fabric, the vertical stitches will cover the raw edge and the side stitches will run parallel with the back of the foot. Pivot *only* after the vertical or horizontal combinations have finished. For instance, in the heavy blanket stitch's 5–4 combination, if you stop midway through the 5 and pivot your fabric, the 5 stitches will *not* sit on top of each other. You *must* count the stitches 5–4, and pivot only after the repeat is finished. This takes a little practice.

If you wish to have a stitch in a particular direction, position the foot in the same direction. In the case of the side stitch, have the back portion of the embroidery foot running at the exact angle you want. For the straight length stitches, the foot must be running alongside the raw edge of the appliqué. Work one stitch at a time, one angle at a time. Always stop with the needle down in your work.

It is best if you stitch slowly for accuracy and learn the rhythm of your stitches (page 28).

Lining up raw edge for perfect stitching

▪ Photo by Deborah Louie

Perfecting Curves, Corners, and Points

How very annoying is it when you are trying to stitch a corner or point with blanket stitching and you overshoot the mark? So annoying! The following techniques need a little practice but will be worth learning.

Circles

1. Draw the shape on test fabric and make some trial runs to make for a lot less unpicking.

2. First, know the rhythm of the stitch you want to use. Is it a 3–2 or 5–4 combination? Adjust the stitch length to suit the appliqué shape. Small circles work well with small stitches and large circles look amazing with large, long stitches.

3. When stitching circles, the main point to consider is that the horizontal side stitches must run parallel to each other. They can look messy if they are not. To achieve perfect results, be sure that the side of the foot is running parallel with the edge of the appliqué before you start stitching.

4. Stitch one repeat of the side and straight stitches and stop with the needle down.

5. Lift the foot lever and pivot (turn) the appliqué shape until the vertical stitch is parallel again. Stitch one repeat only and stop.

It takes time to know when to take your foot off the presser pedal. Some brands of machines make an extra stitch once your foot is off the pedal. In this case, you must release your foot pedal one stitch earlier. This is tricky to do, but stitching slowly makes it possible. You can also do this by pressing the needle up/down button.

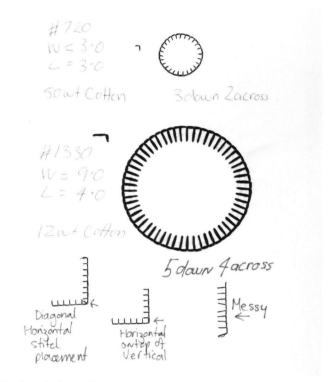

Perfect circles and corners

Corners and Points

When stitching corners, there are a few options. As you get to the corner, the horizontal stitch can either be angled at 45° or run back over the edge again, double stitching it.

If the last vertical stitch looks like it will not be long enough to reach the corner point, adjust the length dial. This adjusted length must then be stitched on the opposite side of the corner point, but remember then to change the length back to the original setting.

As I said before, this takes practice but is very achievable, and you will be delighted with your corners.

Blanket Stitch Variations

By exploring your machine, you may find some variations of blanket stitches. Some common variations are 2 stitches down before the horizontal side stitches or 2 stitches across as I have stitched on Lisa. Another variation is a blanket stitch that graduates in width from narrow to wide.

Various blanket stitches on Lisa

MY FAVORITE: SATIN STITCH PATTERNS

Why Are Satin Stitch Patterns So Useful?

You may think of the satin stitch as just a dense zig-zag that forms a thick, straight-sided line. But most machines can make several decorative patterns that use a satin stitch to fill in repeating shapes such as arrows, balls, and hearts. Double-sided grass is, I have to say, my go-to pattern when I can't think of another pattern to use.

These decorative satin-stitch patterns make a wonderfully strong statement on appliqué, particularly when they are stitched in colored, shiny thread that is a contrast to the color of the fabric.

Satin stitch patterns come in centerline and side-line variations. They are perfect to use when a solid appearance is needed or when you want to draw the eye to a certain section of the flower.

Double-sided grass stitch from Garden Runner

Best Threads for Satin Stitch

Shiny polyester or rayon threads, especially in contrasting colors, create spectacular satin stitch patterns. These threads are flatter than cotton, so the stitches can be adjusted to sit densely close together. Cotton threads are not recommended for satin stitch patterns. They tend to build up, and the embroidery foot can get jammed on top of the stitches if they are too close.

Not all polyester threads are shiny. Avoid regular dress-making polyester threads, as they are dull and look like ordinary cotton thread.

Satin stitch arrows and grass stitch

Photo by Deborah Louie

Stitch Density

When you use fine, shiny polyester thread on most machines, the default length setting (the distance between the stitches) will be too long, making the stitches too far apart and the pattern too open. Try making the length shorter, around 0.20–0.15 on most machines, for a denser stitch that looks wonderful.

Alternatively, if you are using a thicker thread, make the stitch length slightly longer so the stitches will be wider apart to avoid thread buildup and stitch jamming. The stitch length will depend on the roundness and thickness of your thread.

Stitching out your satin stitch patterns in your diary and playing with the stitch length with different thread weights is fun to do. If your bobbin thread starts to come to the top of your stitches, loosen the top thread tension a little (smaller number).

Elongating the Dense Stitches

Once you start to shorten the stitch length on the satin stitch patterns, the shape soon changes. It gets smaller and sometimes it might not be what you want or need. To maintain the pattern when the stitch length is shortened, see if your machine has a feature called *elongation*. On my BERNINA 770 QE, this symbol is a triangle with arrows at the top and bottom to stretch the pattern in percentage amounts. Some machines have a letter *E* on a button, and this shows that the pattern can be elongated ×2 (twice as large), ×3, ×4, ×5, and so on to make the shape very different.

With this feature you now have so many more decorative stitch-pattern options. It is so much fun to see how long and how many more pattern options you have using this elongation feature.

Satin stitch side-line arrows from Bigger Garden Cushion

Various satin stitch patterns from Bigger Garden Cushion

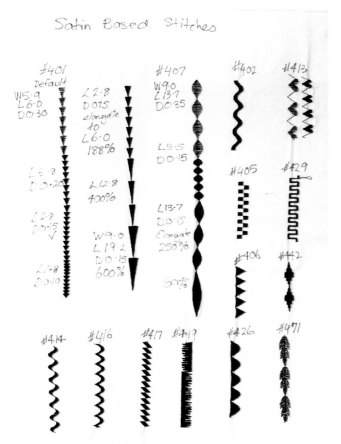

Satin stitches sample sheet

Stitches That Do Not Cover a Straight Edge

On most machines, there are so many beautiful stitches that do not have a straight line, either centered or on the side. It seems a shame not to use them. The great news is we can use these glorious designs in other ways. They can add texture, style, and design inside leaves, petals, and clamshells.

Special Positioning of These Stitches

In many areas of my appliqué, I have space where these stitches can add more life and excitement to the inside of shapes. Adding stitching in a contrasting thread inside the petals and down the center of the larger leaves really adds to the wow factor. This extra detail raises this style of decorative stitching to another level. There is always something to look at and admire, not to mention how wonderful it is to use so many different stitches on one project. To get the full use of your sewing machine's ability is thrilling!

These stitches are way too pretty to ignore and leave out. I find using 12-weight thread in bright, happy colors with these stitches works perfectly to really catch the eye.

Stitching inside petals and leaves found on Garden Runner

As with the other styles of stitches, look in your machine's stitch folders and stitch out all the stitch patterns in your diary. There might be some cross-stitches, some decorative quilting stitches, and perhaps some flowers and leaves running together. Don't forget to write down the machine's setting of width and length as you go. I find that the default setting usually does not need adjusting too much for these stitch patterns.

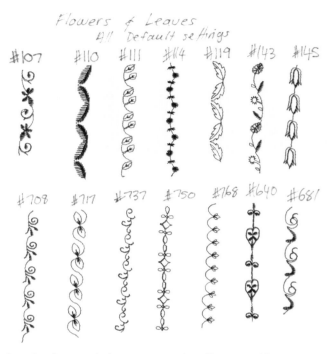

Sample of some stitch patterns used on flowers and leaves

Stitching inside petals of Claire on Little Garden Cushion

Cross-Stitches

Another very pretty range of stitches is cross-stitches. These look so lovely inside petals and inside the larger leaves in 12-weight thread. I do find the default setting for these designs is perfectly balanced and gives a hand-stitched look to my work.

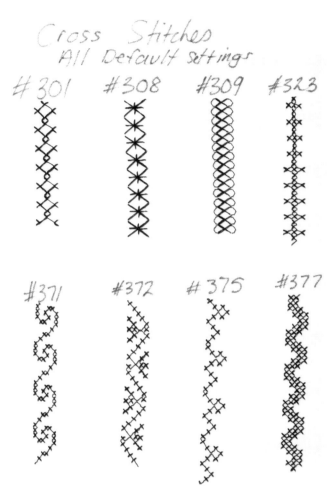

Sample of cross-stitches

DESIGNING YOUR OWN DECORATIVE STITCHES

Combining Decorative Stitches to Make Your Own Patterns

By now, I hope you are enjoying exploring the decorative stitches on your machine and are feeling more confident about using them. Designing or creating your own stitch combinations to make unique patterns is fun and makes your appliqué unique and special.

To start, I suggest you check your sewing machine manual to see how it combines stitches. On my BERNINA 770 QE, I can activate a combination button at the bottom of the screen to add as many different patterns as I wish. They will then stitch out in order one after the other. You can adjust the settings as required and save them in a folder for future use.

Detail of Bigger Garden Cushion, showing star designs combined in many ways

Design Features to Keep in Mind

Combining patterns works well if you consider where a pattern ends and where the next pattern starts. If the two line up in the same needle position, the design will flow nicely from one to the other. I had fun on the flower Daisy using just the star design and combining different combinations of width and length in 12-weight cotton threads.

On Pippy, I used a varied centerline satin oval pattern. Using shiny 40-weight polyester threads, I first made the oval dense with a length of 0.20 and a width of 5.0, and then added a zigzag with a width of 9.0 and a length of 0.10 between the ovals. It is a simple combination of only two different stitches, but one I really like and use often.

Memorizing Patterns

If your machine has the capacity to memorize any stitch that has been changed from the default setting as well as pattern combinations, I suggest you get into the habit of memorizing every new stitch. I keep these memorized stitches in folders on my machine with a new folder for every new project I start. This is efficient and time-saving because I do not have to keep going back and changing settings. This memorizing feature is very important for me to have on a sewing machine and perhaps something for you to keep in mind when you are shopping for a new machine. If you are not sure if you have a memorizing feature, check your manual or visit your dealer for advice.

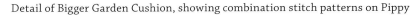

Detail of Bigger Garden Cushion, showing combination stitch patterns on Pippy

SOME GUIDELINES FIRST

Let's quickly go through how to set up your machine for machine appliqué. See full details in How to Set Up Your Machine (page 10).

1. Insert an open-toe embroidery foot, a new size 90 topstitch needle, and white bobbin fill thread in the machine.

2. If possible, select tie-on knots to start and tie-off knots to finish stitching and a foot pivot with the needle down.

3. Place stabilizer under your prepared flower.

4. Start every new stitch pattern on your flower by bringing up the bobbin thread: hold onto the top thread only and place the needle down and then up again.

5. Pull on the top thread until a loop of the bobbin fill thread comes up, and pull it until it is a single thread only.

6. Hold firmly onto the top and bobbin threads, press the pattern begin button to start the pattern from the beginning, and slowly start stitching the stitch pattern.

7. At this stage, it is important to know that you will be stitching only on the raw edges inside the shape. You will stitch the outside edges later, after you place the appliqué elements on the background fabric.

STITCHING STACKED FLOWERS

See Some Guidelines First (previous page) to set up your machine.

Practicing Flower Doreen: Step-by-Step Guide

Prepare the Appliqué Shapes

Cut out and stack the shapes for Doreen (see Preparing Fusible Shapes, page 21).

Fused Doreen ready for stitching

Star Stitching

1. Thread a new size 90 topstitch needle with a colored 12-weight cotton thread from your thread palette (see Choosing a Color Palette of Threads, page 16). I used white.

2. Draw shape 3 onto a spare piece of fabric, called a *test fabric,* and pin stabilizer behind it for support. Name your drawing "test Doreen."

3. Select the star pattern or something similar on your machine. I used stitch pattern 711 on my BERNINA 770 QE, with a width of 5.5 and a length of 5.5. This is a small shape, so only a small star is needed (see Centerline Decorative Stitches, page 33).

4. Slowly stitch out the star pattern on test Doreen to test tension and find the rhythm of the stitch pattern

(page 28). Do this test as many times as necessary to achieve the perfect length and width of the star pattern. See Star Stitch and Adjusting for Variety (page 33) and Testing for Accurate Pattern Repeats (page 34).

5. When you are ready, stitch the pattern onto Doreen, starting with the embroidery foot centered on the raw edge of shape 3.

6. Bring the bobbin thread to the top, stitch the first star with a tie on at the beginning, and stop with the needle down at the end of the star (see Understanding Perfect Stitch-Pattern Placement, page 28).

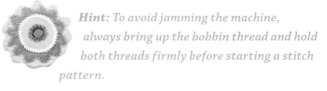

Hint: *To avoid jamming the machine, always bring up the bobbin thread and hold both threads firmly before starting a stitch pattern.*

7. Pivot either at the end of the star or, if needed, in the center of the star before starting the next repeat of the star.

8. Slowly repeat stitching the star pattern around shape 3 until the last star. End with a tie off or, if you prefer, use a self-threading needle to take the starting and finishing threads to the back, knot them together, and cut the excess threads.

First row: Stars on shape 3

Blanket Stitching

1. Thread a new color of 12-weight cotton thread for shape 2. I used hot pink.

2. Draw shape 2 onto the test fabric.

3. Select a medium blanket stitch (page 37) and stitch it out on the test fabric. I have used pattern 720 with a width of 3.0 and a length of 3.0.

4. When you are ready, place the embroidery foot down onto Doreen on the right-hand side of shape 2's raw edge.

5. Holding both threads firmly, stitch one repeat of the blanket stitch (see Counting the Stitches, page 39) and stop with the needle down in the work.

6. Before stitching the next pattern repeat, line up the raw edge with the side of the embroidery foot.

7. Repeat Step 6 for every pattern repeat as you slowly stitch around shape 2. Tie off or knot the threads at the back and cut the excess threads.

Flower Pattern

1. Thread the needle with a shiny, colored 40-weight 100% polyester thread. I used white.

2. Draw shape 1 onto the test fabric and then draw shape 2 inside as it appears on Doreen. Place the foot midway between the edges of the 2 shapes.

3. Select a pretty centerline flower pattern. I used flower pattern stitch 123 with a width of 9.0 and a length of 7.0. Test the pattern for stitch length to achieve a perfect pattern repeat at the end.

4. When you are ready, place the embroidery foot down onto Doreen so it is centered between the raw edges of shapes 2 and 3.

5. Slowly stitch the pattern, staying centered between the raw edges. Tie off or knot the threads at the back and cut the excess threads.

Second row: Blanket stitch on shape 2

Third row: Flower stitch in between the edges of shapes 1 and 2

Add Triple Stitch to the Flower Pattern

Adding a triple stitch in 12-weight cotton thread along the centerline of the flower pattern will add more texture and interest to this row.

1. Thread needle with a 12-weight cotton thread from your thread palette. I used white here.

2. Select a triple stitch (see The Very Useful Triple Stitch, page 32). I have used triple stitch 6 with a length of 4.0.

3. Test the stitch first for tension and rhythm.

4. Place the embroidery foot down onto Doreen so it is centered on the centerline of the flower pattern.

5. Stitch slowly along the centerline of the flower pattern. Tie off or knot the threads at the back and cut the excess threads.

Triple Stitch Around Shape 4

Shape 4 is very small, so I thought all that was needed was a triple stitch in a strong harmonious color.

1. Change the 12-weight cotton thread to a color of your choice. I used purple.

2. Place the embroidery foot down onto Doreen so it is centered on the raw edge of shape 4.

3. With the same stitch length setting that you used for Add Triple Stitch to the Flower Pattern (at left), slowly stitch 1 triple stitch at a time around the small shape. Tie off or knot the threads at the back and cut the excess threads.

Third row: Triple stitch along centerline of flower pattern on shape 1

Fourth row: Triple stitch on shape 4

Hint: *If skipped stitches start to appear, change to a brand-new needle.*

Overlocking Stitch Around Shape 5

For the tiny central shape 5, I used a common utility overlocking stitch. I love that a very common stitch pattern can look unexpectedly good as a brightly colored appliqué stitch pattern.

1. Thread the needle with a shiny, colored 40-weight 100% polyester thread from your thread palette. I used yellow.

2. Draw shape 5 onto the test fabric.

3. Select the overlocking stitch. I used stitch pattern 19 with a width of 5.5 and a length of 2.0, with the straight line covering the raw edge on the left-hand side. See Side-Line Decorative Stitches (page 36) for the difference between left-hand and right-hand–side patterns. Stitch out the pattern on the test fabric.

4. When you are ready, place the embroidery foot down onto Doreen on the left side of shape 5's raw edge.

5. Slowly stitching one pattern at a time, while stopping and pivoting in between, will give perfect results. Tie off or knot the threads at the back and cut the excess threads.

6. If the raw edge is not sufficiently covered, use a triple stitch with the same thread to stitch over it again, again tying off or knotting the threads at the back.

Fifth row: Overlocking stitch on shape 5

Please note that once the stitching is completed, the original size of all the flowers will be slightly reduced; this does not affect the overall project.

Doreen is completed for the time being. Pin Doreen onto a design board or keep in a self-sealing bag until needed.

STITCHING LAYERED FLOWERS

See Some Guidelines First (page 46) to set up your machine.

Practicing Flower Eileen: A Step-by-Step Guide

Preparing the Appliqué Shapes

Cut out and stack the shapes for Eileen (see Preparing Fusible Shapes, page 21).

Fused Eileen, ready to start stitching

Heavy Horizontal Lines Pattern

1. Thread a new size 90 topstitch needle with a 12-weight cotton thread in a color that contrasts the colors in Eileen (see Choosing a Color Palette of Threads, page 16). I used turquoise.

2. Draw a few straight lines and the complete Eileen flower onto a new piece of test fabric, and pin stabilizer behind it for support. Name your drawing "test Eileen."

3. Select a heavy horizontal line pattern or something similar on your machine. I used stitch pattern 1324 on my BERNINA 770 QE with a width of 9.0 and a length of 8.9.

4. Slowly stitch out the heavy horizontal lines pattern along the straight lines on the test fabric to test tension and find the rhythm of the stitch pattern (page 28).

5. Place the embroidery foot down on test Eileen, centering it on the raw edge at the top between shapes 7 and 8.

6. Bring up the bobbin thread by holding onto the top thread only and placing the needle down and then up again.

7. Pull on the top thread until a loop of the bobbin thread comes up, and pull it until it is a single thread only.

8. Hold firmly onto the top and bobbin threads, and slowly stitch the line between the 2 shapes with a tie on at the beginning.

9. At the end of the line, turn Eileen around and, using the same thread, triple stitch with a length of about 4.0 back over this stitching to the beginning, just to be sure the raw edge is covered sufficiently. Tie off or knot the threads at the back and cut the excess threads.

10. When you are ready, stitch the pattern onto Eileen on the raw edges between shapes 7 and 8 and then shapes 5 and 6.

Eileen with heavy horizontal stitching

 Hint: *Trimming threads as you progress will keep your flowers neat and organized.*

Butterfly Flower and Crosses Stitch

1. Thread the needle with 12-weight cotton thread in a color that is complementary to the colors in Eileen. I used magenta.

2. Draw a few straight and small curved lines onto the test fabric.

3. Select a butterfly flower centerline pattern or something similar on your machine. I used stitch pattern 123 on my BERNINA 770 QE with a width of 9.0 and a length of 8.0.

4. On the test fabric, slowly stitch out the pattern around the curved line of shape 5 to test the tension, being careful to stop and pivot after each butterfly flower.

5. When you are ready, stitch the pattern on Eileen, starting with the embroidery foot centered on the raw edge at the top between shapes 3 and 7. Stitch along this raw edge and then along the raw edge between shapes 5 and 2.

6. Select a centerline crosses pattern or something similar on your machine to be stitched in the center of shape 9. I used stitch pattern 1320 on my BERNINA 770 QE with a width of 9.0 and a length of 5.0. Using the same thread, test the stitch pattern first.

7. When you are ready, stitch the pattern onto Eileen.

Eileen with butterfly flower and crosses patterns

Serpentine, Triple, and Cross-Stitches

1. Thread the needle with a 12-weight cotton thread in a dark complementary color. I use dark purple here.

2. Place the embroidery foot down onto test Eileen and stitch a triple stitch with a length of 4.0 or similar along the centerline of the crosses pattern inside shape 9.

3. Serpentine is a common utility stitch and is number 4 on my BERNINA 770 QE. Using a width of 5.5 and a length of 4.0, stitch the pattern on test Eileen along the center of shapes 8 and 6 and, when you are ready, stitch it onto Eileen.

4. In the center of shape 10 on test Eileen, stitch a centerline pattern similar to the cross-stitch I used. This is a small area to work in, so stitch slowly to control the number of repeats.

5. When you are ready, stitch the pattern onto Eileen.

Serpentine, triple, and cross-stitch patterns

 Hint: *If you are stitching satin stitches and the bobbin fill thread comes to the top, reduce the top tension a little (smaller number).*

Heavy Blanket Stitch on Shape 9

1. Thread the needle with a 12-weight cotton thread in a blending color. I used coral red.

2. Select a heavy blanket stitch (page 37). I used pattern 1330 with a width of 3.5 and a length of 3.5.

3. Place the embroidery foot down onto test Eileen on the right-hand side of shape 9's raw edge.

4. Holding both threads firmly, stitch 1 repeat of the blanket stitch (see Counting the Stitches, page 39) and stop with the needle down in the work.

5. Before stitching the next pattern repeat, line up the raw edge with the side of the embroidery foot.

6. Repeat Step 5 for every pattern repeat as you slowly stitch along the side of shape 9, and then lift and move the foot and needle to stitch along the other side of shape 9.

7. When you are ready, stitch the pattern onto Eileen.

8. While you have coral red thread in the machine, select the serpentine pattern used in Step 4, mirror reverse it and stitch it along the center of shapes 8 and 6.

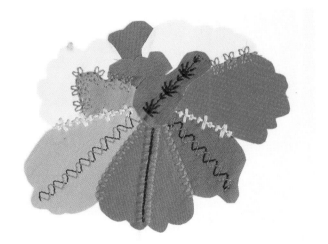

Heavy blanket stitch on shape 9

Satin Serpentine, Satin Zigzag, and Satin Arrows

1. Thread the needle with a light-colored 40-weight 100% polyester thread. I used pink.

2. Select a decorative satin stitch (page 41). I used satin serpentine pattern 414 with a width of 9.0 and a length of 0.20.

3. Place the embroidery foot down onto test Eileen and stitch the pattern along the center of shape 7. When you are ready, stitch the pattern onto Eileen.

4. Select a small arrow stitch pattern or similar centerline pattern. I used pattern 414 (satin arrows facing down) with a width of 5.5 and a length of 0.20.

5. Using the same thread, stitch the pattern onto test Eileen, centering the arrows on the raw edges of shapes 2 and 3 where they overlap shape 1. When you are ready, stitch the pattern onto Eileen.

6. Thread the needle with a dark 40-weight 100% polyester thread. I used dark purple.

7. Select a zigzag stitch, which is usually pattern 2 or close by on most machines. Change the width to 2.0 and the length to 0.20. This will make a very traditional, narrow, and dense centerline satin stitch.

8. Draw a small curved line on the test fabric and stitch the satin stitch pattern along it. This satin stitch is perfect for small areas that are difficult to stitch. The fabric can be slowly pivoted and turned while stitching the pattern, and a lovely dense line of satin stitch will cover the raw edge nicely.

9. Place the embroidery foot down onto test Eileen and stitch the pattern along the edge of shape 4. When you are ready, stitch the pattern onto Eileen.

Adding decorative satin stitch pattern to Eileen

Stars and Triple Stitch Patterns in Silver Thread

1. Thread the needle with a metallic 100% polyester thread or thread of your choice. I used silver.

Hint: Stitch very slowly with metallic thread and use a new size 90 topstitch needle.

2. Select triple stitch again (pattern 6 on my BERNINA 770 QE) with a length of 4.0.

3. Place the embroidery foot down onto test Eileen and stitch some straight lines in areas that need a little more texture, making sure you tie on and off every time. When you are ready, stitch straight lines on Eileen.

4. Draw shape 10 onto some test fabric.

5. Select the star pattern or something similar on your machine. I used stitch pattern 711 on my BERNINA 770 QE with a width of 5.5 and a length of 5.5. Because shape 10 is small, only a small star is needed here. See Centerline Decorative Stitches (page 33).

6. Slowly stitch out the star pattern on the test fabric to test the tension and find the rhythm of the stitch pattern (see Finding the Rhythm of a Stitch Pattern, page 28). Do this test as many times as necessary to achieve the perfect length and width of the star pattern. See Star Stitch and Adjusting for Variety (page 33) and Testing for Accurate Pattern Repeats (page 34).

7. Place the embroidery foot down onto Eileen so it is centered on the raw edge of shape 10.

8. Stitch the first star with a tie on at the beginning and stop with the needle down at the end of the star (see Understanding Perfect Stitch-Pattern Placement, page 28). Pivot and then stitch the next star, working around shape 10.

9. When you are ready, stitch the star pattern onto Eileen.

Addition of silver stitching

Eileen is completed for the time being. Pin Eileen onto a design board or keep in a self-sealing bag until needed.

A GARDEN FULL OF INSPIRATION

In all 4 projects, there are some wonderful opportunities to show your creativity using your decorative stitch patterns on the flowers, leaves, and clamshells.

I have walked you through the stitching process with Doreen and Eileen, and here you can see where I have applied many stitch patterns to other flowers.

If you follow the information for starting, finishing, mirror reversing, changing stitch length and width, using different threads, and changing thread colors, you can't go wrong. You will adore the texture that this will bring to your appliqué.

Bringing color from the flower into my thread color harmonizes and brings a more beautiful look to the appliqué. This can be seen in these 2 Gail flowers.

The oval colors contrast with the petal colors, so bringing the oval colors into the threads on the petals really makes for a good-looking flower.

More appliquéd flowers from Garden Runner

Gail in corals and blues from Garden Runner

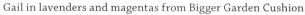
Gail in lavenders and magentas from Bigger Garden Cushion

I try to be efficient when appliquéing. All my flowers, leaves, and clamshells are prepared and pinned to stabilizer before I start to stitch. Then, when I am happy with a particular stitch pattern, I apply that pattern onto a few different flowers and leaves at the same time, changing thread colors during the process to achieve different looks.

Hint: It is easier to rethread the needle with a different thread color to use a particular stitch pattern on numerous flowers, leaves, and clamshells than it is to change stitch patterns while keeping the same thread color.

These are some of my test fabrics for these projects. I am always testing the stitch patterns by changing the length, width, and density, and mirror reversing before I apply them to my projects.

Sample of Deborah's
test fabrics

Decorated leaves

STITCHING INSIDE LEAVES

While you are stitching decorative stitch patterns inside the flowers, stitch them inside some your leaves as well. Having the leaves prepared and pinned on 1 large piece of stabilizer so they're ready to go is efficient and time-saving. Changing the thread color during the process will give a point of difference.

Prepared leaves, ready for stitching

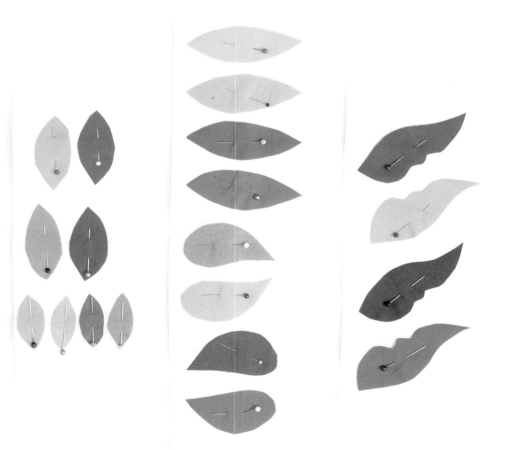

Practicing the Leaves: Step-by-Step Guide

Prepare the Leaves

1. Prepare leaves in a multitude of colors and pin them onto sections of stabilizer (see Preparing Fusible Shapes, page 21).

2. You can stitch the leaves after stitching all the flowers. However, stitching the leaves at the same time as the flowers is more time efficient because it requires fewer thread changes. Line up the embroidery foot with your machine.

3. Whenever a decorative stitch pattern looks beautiful inside of a flower, stitch it out on a leaf or two. Generally, the stitch pattern should be centered on the leaf, leaving a gap of about ¼˝ (0.6cm) at the top and bottom.

Stitching the Leaves

See Some Guidelines First (page 46) to set up your machine.

Chances are you have not used all the stitch patterns on your machine, and this is the perfect chance to enjoy trying them.

Use wide and long stitch patterns for the larger leaves like John, Sam, and Norval.

1. Remember to test new stitch patterns on test fabric before applying them to the leaves.

2. Line up the embroidery foot with the centerline of the leaf. Start stitching ¼″–½″ (0.6–1.3cm) away from the top and finish with a full repeat of the stitch pattern at the bottom of the leaf.

3. Change the color of the thread to get a different look. Both 12-weight cotton and 40-weight 100% polyester threads can be used with satin, side-line, and centerline stitch patterns.

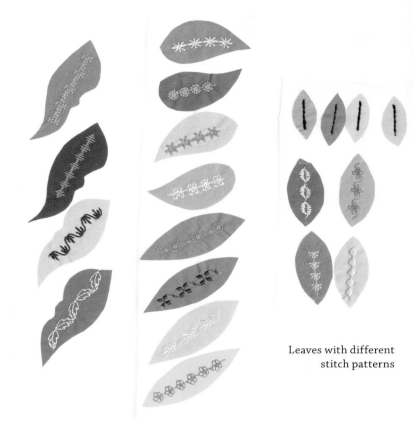

Leaves with different stitch patterns

Black Triple Stitch on Tony Leaves

1. Wind black bobbin fill thread on a bobbin and thread a size 90 topstitch needle with 12-weight black cotton thread.

2. Pin all Tony leaves together on a piece of stabilizer.

3. Select triple stitch (see Add Triple Stitch to the Flower Pattern, page 49). Tie on at the beginning, start stitching ⅛″ (0.3cm) from the top of the leaf along to ⅛″ (0.3cm) from the bottom, and tie off at the end.

4. To work continuously after tying off, lift the embroidery foot and needle and move the next leaf into position under the needle. I call this the "lift-and-drag technique," and you can see it in the photo. Just snip the drag threads from one leaf to the next from the top and back after you have completed all triple stitching.

5. Repeat Step 4 for all leaves, leaving a small section of top and bobbin thread to cut off when they have all been stitched.

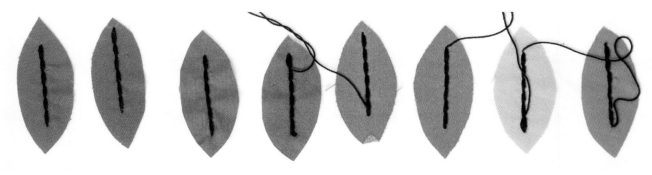

Lift-and-drag triple stitching

STITCHING CLAMSHELLS

Differences Between the Clamshells

There are 2 sizes of clamshells within the Garden series. Both were designed as borders, adding a lovely soft edging that allows all the colors from the flowers and leaves to be repeated and harmonized together.

The Little Garden Cushion Clamshell Border

A full-size clamshell is used along the bottom edge of the Little Garden Cushion and then trimmed even with the finished edge. These clamshells measure 4″ (10.2cm) wide × 4½″ (11.4cm) tall and have a small, separate arch. The different-colored arch is fused onto the top of the full-size clamshell, and the raw edges are covered with decorative stitching. Only the inside raw edges are decoratively stitched at this stage, and they can be done at the same time as the flowers and leaves.

The Garden Runner Clamshell Border

The second size is a smaller clamshell that is used on the Garden Runner clamshell border. These clamshells measure 4″ (10.2cm) long x 3⅛″ (7.9cm) wide. On the Garden Runner border, most clamshells sit neatly on the edge of the border, and some have full-length clamshells behind them. I chose to randomly leave spaces between the clamshells because this allows the border to be fluid and intermingle with the flowers and leaves.

There are no arches inside these small clamshells, so I used a plastic arch template traced from the pattern and a soft, light pencil line to draw a single line onto every clamshell. I then stitched it with a white decorative stitch pattern to add texture.

Garden Runner with clamshell border

■ Photo by Deborah Louie

Full-size clamshells on Little Garden Cushion

Practicing the Clamshells: Step-by-Step Guide

See Some Guidelines First (page 46) to set up your machine.

Prepare the Clamshells

Prepare the clamshells according to the project you are making, and pin onto heavyweight stabilizer only under the arches where the stitching will be (see Preparing Fusible Shapes, page 21).

Stitching the Little Garden Cushion Clamshells

1. For the Little Garden Cushion clamshells, use decorative stitch patterns that will cover the raw edge. You can also place a pattern in between the 2 edges. Use 12-weight cotton and 40-weight 100% polyester threads and enjoy using some fun color combinations. See Learning the Stitches on Your Machine (page 31) for stitch-pattern guidelines.

2. Add a 12-weight cotton thread with a triple stitch in a contrasting colored thread for some eye-catching fun and to reinforce the stitching covering the raw edges.

3. Try a few repeats of a stitch pattern vertically inside the small arch—it can be fun!

Detail of Little Garden Cushion clamshells

Stitching the Garden Runner Clamshells

For the Garden Runner, I used only white 12-weight cotton thread with a multitude of decorative stitch patterns.

1. Remember to add the stabilizer behind each clamshell. Take care to pivot slowly and carefully around the hand-drawn curved line.

2. Cut off the excess threads at the clamshell edge.

3. The clamshells are completed for the time being. Pin them onto a design board or keep them in a sealed bag until needed.

Garden Runner clamshells in stages—drawn, cut, stitched, and stabilizer removed

STABILIZER REMOVAL

What a wonderfully rewarding moment this next stage is! All the decorative stitching has been completed on all flowers, leaves, and clamshells. They are looking amazing, and now we are ready to remove the excess stabilizer from behind them. If your stitching is lovely and flat and not puckered at all, then the stabilizer has performed its job very well.

Method of Cutting Stabilizer

When stabilizer is removed from around the flowers, leaves, and clamshells, it must be left behind the stitching. This is very important because it is needed to support the threads in the stitch patterns. Using a small, sharp pair of scissors, carefully trim away the stabilizer around the flowers, leaves, and clamshells, being careful not to cut their outside edge.

Next, cut as close as you can to the stitch patterns, even cutting at different angles, to remove as much stabilizer as you can. *Remember to leave the stabilizer behind the stitch patterns!* I find that cutting the stabilizer gives a better result than tearing it. I often do this while I am watching TV at night. It can take a while to do, particularly if you are making the Garden Runner or Bigger Garden Cushion.

Once the flowers, leaves, and clamshells have their stabilizer removed, pin them onto a design board or keep them in a sealed bag until needed.

Close-up of stabilizer left behind stitch patterns

Stabilizer trimmed away from Doreen and Eileen

PROJECT ASSEMBLY AND EDGE STITCHING

LAYOUT OF YOUR PROJECT

Be Creative

I love to encourage my students in workshops or regular skill-building classes to be as creative as they wish. My layouts for the 4 projects are only suggestions for you. Please have fun experimenting with different positions for the flowers, leaves, and clamshells, even changing the sizes of the projects. If you have a favorite flower, you now have the skills to design and appliqué it onto your project. Maybe you want more leaves than I have used. That's great! Simply add more leaves and fewer flowers. Make the projects yours.

When you are happy with the number of decorative stitch patterns inside your flowers, leaves, and clamshells and you have removed the stabilizer, it is time to arrange them on your project.

Arranging the Flowers, Leaves, and Clamshells

1. Start with a piece of white paper large enough for your project. Draw a square or rectangle with the same area as the project, for example an 18˝ (45.7cm) square.

Hint: Tabloid (11˝ × 17˝) and A2-sized sketchbooks, available in art stores, have pages that can be easily taped together.

2. Place your larger flowers down where you think they look the best or as shown in the project layout diagrams.

3. The flowers and leaves are connected to stems that I call *vines*. Draw a vine line going from the bottom of each flower to the clamshell border or edge of the area. A smooth curved line is best. These are the *main vines*.

4. Place smaller flowers in position and draw a vine line from each one to the main vine. I call these the *side vines*.

5. Take a photo and see if you have a nice balance of flowers and colors. Rearrange them and retake the photo as many times as necessary until you are happy with your layout.

6. Place the leaves in the empty spaces around the flowers. You should now see your composition taking shape with a lovely distribution of flowers, leaves, and color.

7. Take another photo and check again for balance. Repeat this step until you are happy with your layout.

Appliqué pinned into position on paper pattern

■ Photo by Deborah Louie

Optional: Marking the Base Fabric

At this point, I find it helpful to make a full-size pattern for the layout of my appliqué. I do this for all my projects.

1. Remove the appliqué shapes from the paper.

2. Photocopy the pattern drawings of the flowers and leaves in your project, cut them out, and glue them in position onto the paper in the same position you have captured in your photographs. This makes a full-size pattern sheet.

3. Place the background fabric on top of the full-size pattern and, using a dark, soft pencil like a 2B pencil, mark the vine lines. Then trace the outside lines of every flower and leaf, but ¼″ (6mm) inside the outer line, not on the line. The

A copy of the full-size pattern sheet for Bigger Garden Cushion

flowers and leaves have pulled in a little during stitching, and you don't want your pencil lines to show on the background fabric in the finished project. A lightbox is useful for this step.

PREPARING AND STITCHING THE VINES

Make your own vines using a ¼″ (6mm) bias-tape tool, purchase pre-fused bias tape, or use a heavy machine chain stitch to mimic a hand-embroidered vine.

Preparing Bias Vines

You can use ¼″ (6mm) bias tape backed with fusible web for the vines. It is readily available in a variety of colors at most quilt stores. Or you might prefer to make your own bias tape. Cut ½″ (1.3cm)-wide bias strips so that they are easy to curve. Pull the strips through the bias maker and press slowly. Press ¼″ (6mm) fusible web onto the wrong side just before you use them.

How to Apply Fusible Bias Tape

1. Measure the length of each side vine and cut the fusible bias tape ¼″ (6mm) longer. Remove the paper backing from the fusible, lay the bias tape on the drawn line, and slowly press. If you prefer to add droplets of Roxane's Glue-Baste-It instead of the fusible, please use your preferred method.

2. Measure the main vines and cut the fusible bias tape 1″ longer. Remove the paper backing from the bias tape. Starting at the top of the project or at the base of a flower, lay it on the drawn line and slowly press, making sure the bias tape goes over the top of the edge of the side vines. There should be only a tiny allowance for tucking the end of the vine under the flower. Too much overlap and the edge of the flower will be bulky.

Hint: The left hand carefully curves the bias while the right hand follows closely and presses with a small, hot iron.

Position of hands while pressing bias tape

Stitching the Vines

The vines that connect the flowers and leaves are stitched in a variety of ways on my projects. Any of these techniques can be interchanged within the projects.

It is best to stitch the vines before you put the appliqué flowers and leaf pieces on the background fabric. Stitch right up to the marked flower, leaf, and clamshell outer lines. When you place the appliqué pieces later, you can position them perfectly with a very small overlap of the vines.

Blind Hem Stitching the Vines

Finding the Perfect Blind Hem Stitch Setting

Blind hem or invisible stitching is very effective when you want a no-show stitch on your appliqué to emulate hand-stitched needle-turn appliqué. My hand-stitched needle-turn skills are nonexistent, so I'm grateful that my sewing machine can do a beautiful blind hem stitch.

You are still appliquéing, so keep the bobbin fill thread in the bobbin.

Hint: When you are blind hem stitching, use white bobbin fill thread for a light-colored background fabric and black bobbin fill thread for a dark background fabric.

The blind hem stitch is usually found in the utility stitch section at the front of your machine. On my BERNINA 770 QE, it is stitch pattern 3. The sequence or rhythm of the stitch pattern is 2 straight stitches on the left side then a large zigzag, also on the left side. The default settings need a huge change to make a tiny stitch. See Finding the Rhythm of a Stitch Pattern (page 28).

First, I mirror reverse the stitch because the straight stitches need to be on the right-hand side of the zigzag. If possible, take the needle position to the far right-hand side of the embroidery foot. Then I change the length to 1.00 and the width to 0.60, producing a tiny blind hem stitch. Perfect!

Stitch out your blind hem stitch on a test fabric and keep it in your stitch diary for future reference.

If your make and model of machine does not have a blind hem stitch that can be finely adjusted, try the single blanket stitch. When it is changed to a very small width and length setting, it usually gives an excellent result.

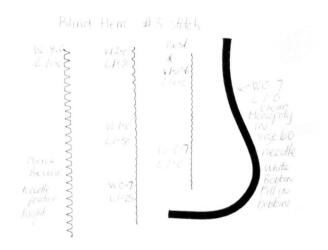

Stitch chart of blind hem stitching sizes

Setting Up for Blind Hem Stitching

Let's go through how to set up your machine for blind hem machine appliqué.

1. Insert an open-toe embroidery foot, a new size 60 sharps needle, and white bobbin fill thread in the machine.

2. If possible, select tie-on knots to start and tie-off knots to finish stitching, and a foot pivot with the needle down.

3. Place small strips of stabilizer behind the background fabric under your bias vines.

4. Thread the needle with a clear polyester thread (I recommend MonoPoly by Superior). You might have to hand thread the needle, as most automatic needle threaders will not thread a size 60 fine needle.

5. Reduce the top thread tension a little (smaller number).

6. To start, bring up the bobbin thread by holding onto the top thread only and placing the needle down and then up again.

7. Pull on the top thread until a loop of the bobbin fill thread comes up and pull it until it is a single thread only.

Hint: *MonoPoly thread (by Superior) is a clear polyester thread that is slightly elastic and can be pressed with an iron, unlike nylon thread, which cannot be pressed.*

Using the Blind Hem Stitch

Hold firmly onto the top and bobbin threads and place the embroidery foot just a fraction (a needle width) off the right-hand edge of the bias strip at the top. With a blind hem stitch pattern, the straight stitches sit on the background fabric and the tiny zigzag stitches come across and land on the edge of the bias strip. If the zigzag is visible, make the width narrower. Place the needle position all the way to the right if possible.

1. Stitch slowly all the way down the right-hand side of the bias strip; then turn and stitch back along the other side, stopping to pivot when necessary. Stitch slowly for accuracy.

2. When you come to a side vine that needs stitching, stop at the corner, pivot, stitch to the end of the side vine, pivot, stitch the tiny end of the vine, pivot, and stitch back to the main vine.

3. When all blind hem stitching is complete, carefully cut away the stabilizer, remembering to leave it behind the stitching for support, and then press.

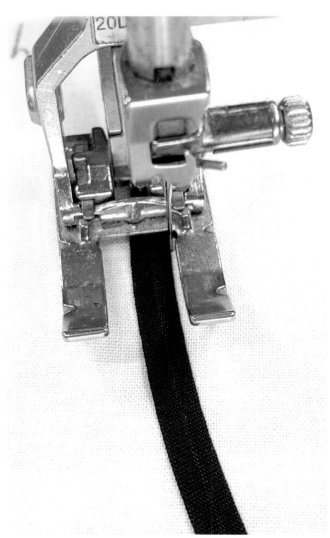

Placement of embroidery foot for blind hem stitching

Photo by Deborah Louie

Topstitching the Vines

For some extra detail on the Garden Runner, I top-stitched the vines with a light-blue 12-weight cotton thread. This topstitch is a straight-stitch pattern. On my BERNINA 770 QE, it is stitch pattern 1 with a length of 3.50, making it a long, well-defined stitch.

The trick here is to have the needle on the far right-hand side of the bias strip. Do this by either changing the needle position or using your width button so that only a small amount of bias is showing when the embroidery foot is down.

Trial topstitch on your test fabric using a variety of stitch lengths and needle positions, and keep it in your diary for future reference.

The guidelines for topstitching are the same as for blind hem stitching, except that you have to use a size 90 topstitch needle with 12-weight cotton thread and black bobbin fill thread in the bobbin.

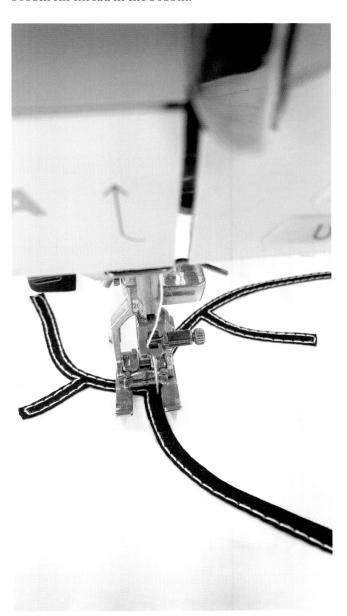

Placement of embroidery foot for topstitching

▪ Photo by Deborah Louie

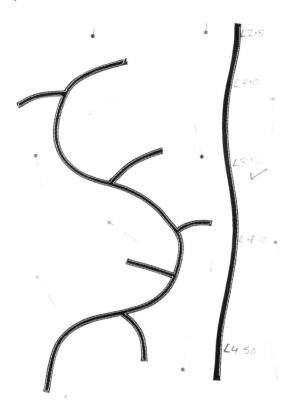

Topstitching on test fabric

Serpentine Stitching the Vines

Why not replace the straight topstitch with a zigzag serpentine stitch? It is a utility stitch commonly found on the front of sewing machines, and the Garden place mats have it on their bias stems.

The serpentine stitch is pattern 4 on my BERNINA 770 QE with a width of 3.0 and a length of 0.50. I used white bobbin fill thread in the bobbin and white 12-weight cotton thread in a size 90 topstitch needle.

1. Simply center the embroidery foot on the bias strip and stitch from the top to the bottom. It is important to note that the serpentine stitch does not travel well around corners. For best results, use it on slight curves and straight bias strips.

This stitch does not cover the edges but is simply centered on the bias strip. No need to add another stitch to cover the edges.

2. Carefully cut away the stabilizer, remembering to leave it behind the stitching for support, and then press.

Serpentine on black bias strips of Doreen

Chain Stitching the Vines

For a different look for the vines on the Bigger Garden Cushion, I used a machine chain stitch (page 33) in lieu of bias-tape vines. When chain stitching with 12-weight thread, the stitch pattern looks like a very heavy straight stitch. On my BERNINA 770 QE, it is pattern 713, and the rhythm of the stitch is 7 times back and forth over the same stitch, resulting in a very thick hand-stitched look, which I love.

If your machine does not have a stitch as thick as chain stitch, then use the triple stitch (page 32).

1. With black bobbin fill thread in the bobbin, heavy 12-weight black cotton thread in the top, a stitch length of 4.5, and using the embroidery foot, stitch very slowly along your drawn line, making sure that the 7 stitches stay on top of each other. Tie off at the beginning and end, or thread through to the back, knot, and cut the threads.

2. While stitching a main vine, it is easy to turn and stitch each side vine as you come to it and then continue stitching the main vine. Switch to a normal straight stitch with the same length to stitch back over the side vine, then switch back to chain stitch to continue along the main vine. Have these 2 stitches memorized for easy access. Some machines will hold your setting in memory, but others will not.

3. Carefully cut away the stabilizer, remembering to leave it behind the stitching for support, and then press.

Chain-stitched vines

■ Photo by Deborah Louie

PLACING APPLIQUÉ SHAPES ON THE BACKGROUND

This is the most exciting time: when you are placing your beautiful and decoratively stitched flowers onto the background fabric. All your hard work is starting to come together! The decorative stitch patterns look amazing, the stabilizer has been removed, and you are now ready to place flowers onto the background fabric.

Add the Larger Flowers

1. At this stage, your background fabric has the vines stitched in place. Lightly press it and place it on a flat pressing surface.

2. If you have made a pattern sheet, place it under the background fabric.

3. Following the lines of your pattern, press each larger flower into position on the background fabric, making sure that it covers a small section of any bias vines connected to it.

4. Cover the flowers with an appliqué pressing sheet, or a piece of parchment or baking paper, and press them, being careful not to overheat and scorch the fabric and threads.

5. If the flowers do not adhere to the fabric, lightly spray temporary adhesive onto the wrong side or use washable basting glue to help them adhere, one flower at a time. Use tweezers to place each flower into position and press into place.

Photo by Deborah Louie

Add the Smaller Flowers

Place the smaller flowers onto the background fabric and press into place. Please do not be concerned if the positioning is different from my projects. Allow your work to talk to you.

■ Photo by Deborah Louie

Add the Leaves

Add the leaves now, making sure that they butt up to the edge of the bias vines, and press them into position. If at this stage your work is looking too sparse, you could make a few more leaves of different sizes and colors. If it is looking too busy, then take some leaves away. Once again, make your project your own.

Addition of all flowers, leaves, and clamshells on runner

■ Photo by Deborah Louie

Add the Clamshells

All clamshells in both the Little Garden Cushion and the Garden Runner projects butt up next to each other in a row. When the clamshells are layered on top of each other, they have a slight ¹⁄₁₆″ (2mm) overlap of the bottom row over the top row.

1. Place all the clamshells carefully into position, making sure they butt up next to each other at their widest point and overlap where necessary.

2. Press with an appliqué pressing sheet or a piece of parchment or baking paper over the clamshells to protect the stitching. Remember to use the temporary basting spray or washable glue if they are not adhering properly.

Little Garden Cushion clamshells in an overlapping position

STITCHING THE APPLIQUÉ EDGES

As the inner flowers, leaves, and clamshells are already beautifully stitched with decorative patterns, only the outer raw edges need stitching at this point. You have two goals—to stitch the outer edge of the shapes to the background and to further define and decorate them. You can accomplish both at the same time with free-motion stitching.

EDGE BASTING APPLIQUÉ

Why Edge Baste?

Have you ever tried to machine appliqué on a project and, as you are stitching and turning the fabric, the appliquéd pieces move or fall off the background fabric? This has happened to me, and it is very annoying. So I started to edge baste my appliqué onto the background fabric before doing the final outside-edge stitching. This was such an effective solution that I edge baste all my appliqué projects now.

Edge basting done in free-motion–stitching mode is easy to do because there is no turning of your work. Simply start at the top of the piece and stitch around all the shapes down to the bottom; then turn your work and stitch again from top to bottom. I will guide you through the process.

Use a clear polyester thread (I recommend MonoPoly by Superior). Its job is to secure the appliquéd pieces onto the background fabric. It will not be visible on the finished project because it will be covered by the colored thread used in the color-on-color sketch-edge appliqué stitching that follows it.

Free-motion foot and edge basting appliqué

■ Photo by Deborah Louie

Sewing Instructions for Edge Basting

Stabilize First

Place a large piece of stabilizer on the wrong side of the background fabric and pin them together with safety pins from the center out to the edges. If necessary, you can overlap sections of stabilizer.

Setting Up Your Machine

1. Attach a closed-toe free-motion foot onto the machine. Do not use an open-toe foot because it can get caught on the decorative stitches.

2. Lower, drop, or cover the feed dogs.

3. Insert white bobbin fill thread (because the background is a light color), a new size 90 topstitch needle, and a straight-stitch plate (if you have one).

4. Thread MonoPoly in the needle, making sure the cone is standing up vertically with no tension on the cone. Reduce the top thread tension a little (smaller number).

5. Select a straight stitch. There is no need to select a stitch length because the feed dogs are lowered.

6. Set the machine to medium/slow speed and to stop with the needle-down.

Practicing Edge Basting

1. Practice first: Draw a few flowers and leaves on a piece of stabilized test fabric.

2. Place the free-motion foot down on the fabric.

3. Bring up the bobbin thread as before and hold both the bobbin and top threads firmly.

4. With the machine motor in slow speed, press the foot pedal all the way down and slowly move the fabric. If you can't change the needle motor speed, press down on the foot pedal about a third of the way only.

5. With thumbs together, frame your hands around the free-motion foot. Try to drop your shoulders and move the fabric smoothly. Practice until you feel comfortable moving the fabric with your hands. This takes time to get used to if you are new to free-motion stitching.

I wear textured multipurpose gloves while free-motion stitching. These gloves have a thick, textured rubber base that grips onto the fabric very well. I purchase them at a hardware store.

6. It is very important to stop moving your hands and the needle when you are uncomfortable. Stitch within an area of only 3–4 square inches (7.6–10.2 square centimeters); then stop with the needle-down and reframe your hands around the next closest area.

7. To start and stop with tie on and tie off, simply stitch a few times without moving the fabric.

Hint: *I press my left foot down on the foot pedal all the way to the floor* but *change the speed of the machine to achieve the required needle speed. This is a good way to learn how to achieve perfect stitch length.*

Edge Basting the Flowers and Leaves

Aim for the stitching to be just a fraction inside the outer edges of the flowers, leaves, and clamshells. This stitching is not needed inside the appliqué because you have already achieved that with your decorative stitch patterns.

Stitch around the outer edge of one flower, and then lift and drag to the next flower or leaf. See Black Triple Stitch on Tony Leaves, Step 3 (page 59).

Work on the right-hand side of the project and meander down to the bottom, lifting and dragging when necessary. Trim the threads, turn your work so that it is upside down, and stitch again from top to bottom.

The length of your stitches does not matter because they will be covered by the color-on-color sketch-edge stitching that follows them.

Hint: Never have any more than half of a project under the arm of the machine, and always stitch top to bottom when free-motion stitching.

Sample of edge-baste stitching on leaf
■ Photo by Deborah Louie

Edge Basting the Clamshell Borders

To edge baste the clamshells, turn the fabric so the clamshells are running from top to bottom along the right-hand side of your project. Frame your hands around a clamshell and stitch just inside the edge, and then stop and reframe your hands around the next clamshell. Repeat this process on the clamshells all the way to the bottom; then stop with the needle down, turn, and stitch down to the bottom again, one clamshell at a time.

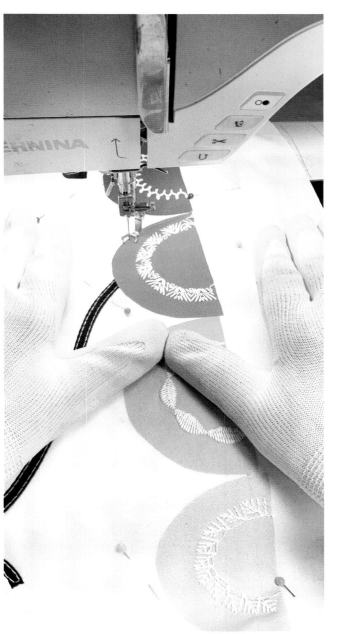

■ Photo by Deborah Louie

SKETCH-EDGE APPLIQUÉ

Why Sketch-Edge Appliqué?

Sketch-edge appliqué is the final stitching on the flowers and leaves before quilting your project. Because they have all been basted, you can now sketch on their outside edges very efficiently by working on one fabric color at a time across the whole project. Like edge basting, this is also done as free-motion stitching.

This adds even more texture to your project, and it is so much easier to do it now rather than later at the quilting stage when your project is heavier to handle. What a fantastic bonus!

Close-up of Rebecca, showing sketched edge and added texture

Which Threads to Use

With sketch-edge appliqué, I use only shiny 100% polyester threads because they are lustrous, strong, and lie flat on the appliqué. These same threads are used for satin-based decorative stitch patterns and for background filler quilting. At this stage, keep bobbin fill thread in the bobbin. Rayon threads also give a beautiful edge but are a little softer and break more easily than polyester. If you want to use them, you can overcome this problem by stitching more slowly.

Select shiny polyester threads that match as closely as possible to all the fabric colors of the outer edges of your flowers and leaves. Put them together in a basket or box. This will save time later.

Setting Up Your Machine

Refer to the instructions in Edge Basting Appliqué (page 73), but instead of using MonoPoly thread, use a shiny colored 100% polyester thread and change the closed-toe foot to an open-toe free-motion foot for better viewing of the raw edge.

Practicing Sketch-Edge Appliqué

Sketch-edge appliqué is like edge basting, except that you will be stitching 3 times over the raw edge in a colored thread that matches the fabric color.

Use your stabilized test fabric with some drawn flowers and leaves to practice. It can take a little time to feel comfortable with sketch-edge appliqué. There is a nice, smooth rhythm between your hands, the machine, and the stitching when you can confidently stitch 1, 2, 3, stop, reframe, 1, 2, 3, stop, reframe, and so on. If you sketch too fast, you can feel out of control very quickly.

When you use a slow-to-medium speed with slow, smooth hands, you should feel comfortable and very much in control.

1. Stitch the raw edge only 2″ at a time, moving the fabric with your hands slowly forward, back, and forward so that the stitches sit on top of each other as you say to yourself, "forward, back, forward, stop" or "1, 2, 3, stop."

2. If the raw edge is nicely covered, move along to the next 2″ of the raw edge and stitch 1, 2, 3, stop.

3. If the edge is not covered thickly enough or you didn't get close enough to the edge, stitch a few more times, up to a total of 5 or 7 times, over the same edge. Remember you are using a flat thread. Layers of a round cotton thread would form a thick edge of stitching, but layers of this flat thread work well because they sit flat on the edge. Because you are in free-motion mode on the machine, you can move the fabric in any direction freely.

Sketch-Edge Appliquéing the Flowers and Leaves

1. Choose a thread to match the fabric color on the edge of one flower and sketch the edge. When finished, lift and drag to the edge of another flower or leaf of the same color, sketch it, and lift and drag again. Every time you start and stop, slow down your hands to get small, close anchoring stitches.

2. Lift and drag all over your project with your first thread color until all the edges in this color have been sketched. Snip all dragged top and bobbin threads. There is no need to bring the threads through to the back and knot them because the anchoring stitches will hold the threads firmly.

3. Change to a different color of thread and sketch all edges of that color. Some of the layered flowers have numerous edges in different colors. There is no need to change the colored thread numerous times while sketching on one flower. The basting holds the flower securely on the background fabric so you can sketch the different-colored edges of the flower at different times. This saves a lot of time and is very efficient and rewarding.

Lozzy sketched with one color of thread at a time

DRAMATIC KEY-LINE STITCHING

I thought I had finished the decorative stitching for the floral part of the Bigger Garden Cushion, but I decided it was just not finished. I had to do more. What should I do? Should I stitch a fine black line on the background fabric very close to the outside edge of the flowers and leaves to enhance, draw attention to, and sharpen their appearance? I made trial stitches on a flower or two using 12-weight cotton thread and free-motion stitching, and I added some tendrils along the way. Well, I'm really glad I did because I love it. It's just what my project needed. The choice to add key-line stitching to your projects is entirely up to you.

Setting Up Your Machine

1. Insert an open-toe free-motion foot, a new size 90 topstitch needle, and a straight stitch plate (if you have one). Lower, drop, or cover the feed dogs.

2. Use black bobbin fill thread and 12-weight cotton thread in black or a color of your choice.

3. Select a slow speed, stop with the needle down, and use a straight stitch. No stitch length is needed.

4. Test the tension on some stabilized test fabric and loosen the top tension a little if necessary (smaller number).

Close-up of key-line stitching around Lisa flower and leaves

How to Do Key-Line Stitching

When you are using heavy 12-weight thread, you must stitch slowly. If you stitch too quickly, the thread will break.

1. Always bring up the bobbin thread to the top and hold both threads firmly at the start. Move your hands slowly and smoothly, stopping frequently with the needle down to reframe your hands around the free-motion foot. It is best not to backtrack (to stitch back over a line a second time).

2. Always stitch around a flower or leaf in one direction to finish back at the start; then lift and drag to the next flower or leaf. Where flowers and leaves are very close together, lift and drag the project 6˝ to the left and then bring it back. This will give you enough bobbin and top thread to tie off the threads later.

3. Add a long, soft tendril by stitching out, curling the end, stopping with the needle down, and stitching back. The line should be soft and relaxed, not trying to come back over the existing line at all, but some overlapping looks good. Tendrils between petals or next to leaves add a more fluid look to the project.

Key-line stitching and lift-and-drag threads ready to thread to the back

■ Photo by Deborah Louie

Finishing Off the Stitching

When the key-line stitching is complete, there are many threads to take to the back, knot, and cut off to make your project look neat and beautiful. This takes time; using a self-threading needle helps speed up the process. I promise it will be worth it.

Back view of knotting and cutting off key-line threads

■ Photo by Deborah Louie

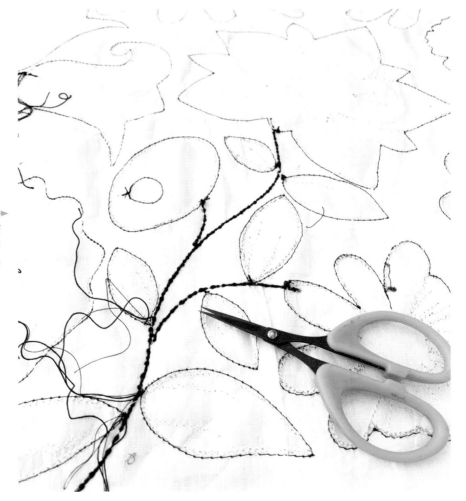

COMPLETING THE CLAMSHELLS

The edges of the clamshells need a bold, symmetrical design, so I use a decorative stitch pattern instead of a free-motion stitch to cover the slight overlapping between clams. You can stitch this at the end or before you sketch-edge stitch the flowers and leaves.

Whenever you are using satin decorative-stitch patterns, always remember to use a shiny polyester thread and adjust the length of the stitches for perfect stitch density (page 42).

Satin Stitch Round Balls Pattern

The clamshells on the Little Garden Cushion are stitched with a satin stitch round balls pattern in contrasting thread. Because the curves on the clamshells are tight, remember to stitch slowly and pivot carefully at the end of every pattern repeat. The clamshells do not necessarily have to be an even distance apart, so the exact number of balls on each can vary. If you are close to the join from one ball to the next at a corner point but the ball will be too big, just hold back the fabric a little to make a shorter pattern. See Centerline Decorative Stitches (page 33).

Double-Sided Grass Stitch

A relaxed and symmetrical double-sided satin grass-stitch pattern is stitched on the curved edge of the Garden Runner clamshells. Using only white thread both inside and on the edge of the clamshells highlights the stitch patterns and makes an elegant statement.

1. Stitch the curved edges of the inner row of clamshells first, lifting and dragging from one to the other, and trim the threads.

2. Work from top to bottom along the right-hand side of the runner, stitching the curved edges of the outer row of clamshells and pivoting with the needle down after every pattern repeat. When crossing from one clamshell to the next, make a tiny lift and drag with a slight overlap.

Cross-over for clamshells

■ Photo by Deborah Louie

Check your lift-and-drag threads. If they are causing puckering, they will need to be cut and tied. If they are loose, no cutting is needed. Remove the stabilizer except where it must be left behind the stitching for support. Cut close to the stitching with small sharp scissors. Take extra care not to cut the background fabric. This task is time-consuming and messy, and I usually have stabilizer from one end of the house to the other.

Turn your project right side up and press, making sure to cover it with a cloth to protect the decorative stitching. Lay it flat or pin it onto a design wall until needed.

A huge congratulations from me to you. How wonderful it is for you to have a full understanding and love of your sewing machine!

Bigger Garden Cushion with stabilizer removed and mess it leaves in my studio

▉ Photo by Deborah Louie

Reverse side of Bigger Garden Cushion with loose lift-and-drag threads and ready to have stabilizer removed

 Photo by Deborah Louie

QUILTING YOUR
PROJECT

For me, machine appliqué tells one-half of the story of a quilt or project and the machine quilting tells the other half, so much so that one is lost without the other. Quilting adds so much texture and personality to your work, drawing attention to the fabulous decorative stitching.

Free-motion ditch quilting combined with a dense background filler has a magical effect on all the appliquéd flowers, leaves, and clamshells, making them pop up off the background fabric. I will walk you through how to use your domestic machine to quilt all four projects.

Close-up of quilting and way it draws attention to appliqué

Preparing the Backing Fabric

The backing fabric for each project should be 2″–3″ (5.1–7.6cm) larger than the top on all 4 sides. Lay the backing fabric on a large, flat surface like a table, with the wrong side of the fabric facing up. Apply strips of paper masking tape firmly without gaps along all sides of the fabric. Be mindful to line up the side, top, and bottom edges of the backing fabric with the edges of the table or other surface.

The color of the backing fabric works well when it is matched to the top thread. In the case of the Garden Runner, white thread is used for the background quilting, and so a white-based backing fabric with small dots or small-scale flowers would work well. I have used a very light gray-and-white print. The cushions have a separate backing fabric that can be quilted or left unquilted. This is your choice.

Choosing Your Batting

I have used a white medium-loft 100% polyester batting with scrim for the four projects. Scrimmed batting has a fine base of nonwoven interfacing that has been needle-punched into the batting. This makes the batting strong and very durable. If a low-loft batting such as cotton is used, the appliqué will not pop as well.

Polyester batting, safety pins, basting spray, and tape

Basting Your Project

1. Spray an even coverage of temporary basting spray over the backing fabric; then lay the batting, scrim face-down, carefully working from the top end to the bottom.

2. Lay your freshly pressed project directly onto the batting. Smooth it out and straighten it.

3. Roll up half of the project toward the center, exposing the batting.

4. Spray an even coverage of temporary basting spray over half of the batting.

5. Place both hands under the roll of your project and work slowly, a little at a time, to smooth out the project on top from the center out to the edge.

6. Repeat this process on the other half.

7. Remove the tape from the backing fabric and press the top and back of the project to dry the spray. Protect the decorative stitching on the top with a pressing cloth.

Pinning Your Project

If you prefer to pin baste your project, place the batting firmly down onto the backing fabric and then your freshly pressed project on top of the batting. Starting in the center and working out to the sides, top, and bottom, carefully pin the 3 layers together, smoothing out the background fabric carefully. Avoid placing pins inside the appliquéd areas, instead placing them only in the background areas. When the pinning is finished, remove the tape.

WALKING-FOOT QUILTING

Using your walking foot, you can make beautiful quilting lines by just following a line. This is easiest with straight lines or gentle curves where you don't have to turn the project too often.

Quilting a Crosshatch Design

How beautiful is a classic crosshatch quilting design? When I saw that the diagonal lines in the Doreen's Place Mat (page 98) gingham check would reveal evenly spaced quilting lines, I knew I should "let the fabric guide the quilting." No need to mark—just turn the fabric on the diagonal and quilt from one corner of a dark gray square to the next. But you could always use the 45° guidelines on a quilting ruler to mark the lines.

Gingham check print and guidelines

■ Photo by Deborah Louie

Hint: "It's a walking foot, not a running foot … quilt slowly."

Setting Up Your Machine

1. Attach an open-toe walking foot with the feed dogs up.

2. Insert a new size 90 topstitch needle, 12-weight cotton thread in the top, and 50-weight cotton thread in the bobbin.

3. Select a long, straight stitch with a length of 4.5. Test the tension on testing fabric.

4. Using a pencil, mark out the size of the area to be quilted. On the 18″ × 12″ (45.72 × 30.5cm) place mats, you would mark 17½″ × 11½″ (44.5 × 29.2cm). When quilting on a solid background fabric, draw up a 1″ (2.5cm) regular crosshatch with a stencil or a ruler and pencil.

Quilting Directional Plan

1. Starting stitching with a tie-on stitch at the corner marked 1 on the diagram, and slowly quilt to the end of this black-colored row.

2. Stitch along the ¼″ (6mm) binding area outside the pencil-marked area to meet row 2, and stitch along row 2 in the opposite direction.

3. Continue quilting along the black rows to the corner according to the diagram. Tie off and cut the threads.

4. Turn the place mat counterclockwise and quilt the pink rows from the center out to the corner.

5. Repeat Step 4 for the blue rows and then for the green rows.

6. Travel from one row to the next in the ¼″ (6mm) area where the peeper and binding will be placed. Leave the project flat, ready for the next stage.

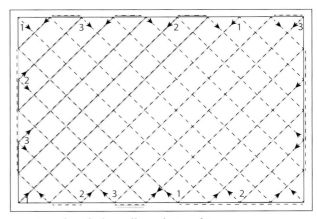

Directional guide for walking-foot quilting

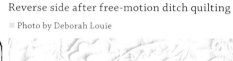

FREE-MOTION DITCH QUILTING

What Is Ditch Quilting?

Quilting-in-the-ditch is often thought of as synonymous with walking-foot quilting. In my view, ditch quilting is a technique, not a foot on your machine. I free-motion ditch quilt all seams or lines, whether they are straight or curved. Consider the appliquéd flowers, both layered and stacked types. Where one shape sits on top of or next to another shape, the 2 shapes need division, and so that is a ditch-quilting opportunity.

I love the "abstract wholecloth quilt" look of the Bigger Garden Cushion's reverse side. It's a shame that this will never be seen, as it will be inside the cushion.

Front view of Bigger Garden Cushion after free-motion ditch quilting
■ Photo by Deborah Louie

Reverse side after free-motion ditch quilting
■ Photo by Deborah Louie

Ditch Quilting the Flowers

Let's look at flower Eileen. Every petal is ditch quilted and sitting flat. I start by quilting around a flower or leaf, with the quilting sitting as close as possible to the edge. Then I quilt around the petal shapes and the most decorative stitch patterns within them. This high level of detail is so eye-catching that you can't see the stitching, only its effects.

Ditch quilting inside Eileen

Which Threads to Use

Use a clear polyester thread (I recommend MonoPoly by Superior) in the needle so that you cannot see the stitches, only their effects in making the patterns sit flat. Use shiny 100% polyester thread with a color to match the background fabric in the bobbin. Test the stitching and adjust the tension if necessary before venturing on to your project.

■ Photo by Deborah Louie

Stitching-in-the-Ditch

The movements will be familiar to you by now, since the stitching is similar to what you did in edge basting appliqué (page 73) and sketch-edge appliqué (page 76).

1. Set up your machine with a closed-toe free-motion foot, feed dogs down, a straight stitch, and set the needle to stop in the down position Loosen the top tension if necessary (smaller number).

2. Set the machine speed to slow. Move the fabric slowly and carefully to quilt-in-the-ditch as close as possible to the outside edge of the flowers and leaves. Travel inside each flower and leaf before moving on to the next one.

Backtracking and doubling up to work continuously is fine and will not show at all. If necessary, lift and drag threads from one area to the next.

3. To start and finish, move the fabric very slowly to get small, closely stitched running stitches; then cut the top and back threads.

BACKGROUND QUILTING: PEBBLES, TEARDROPS, AND MORE

After the free-motion ditch quilting has been completed, your project will be flat, secure, and looking fabulous. You can finish your project there, or you can add even more texture by free-motion quilting some background fillers onto the background fabric, as I have.

On the Little Garden Cushion, the background quilting begins with pebbles along the top of the clamshell border, meanders in between the flowers and leaves, and finishes with wavy lines in the sky. It is all done as free-motion quilting. For machine set up, see Free-Motion Ditch Quilting (page 86). Shiny sky-blue 100% polyester thread was used in both the needle and the bobbin. This is free-form, soft, and relaxed meandering quilting that produces flowing lines wherever you think they are needed.

Free-motion quilted pebbles and meandering

Pebble Background Quilting

Smooth, slow hand movement and a medium to fast needle are important here because small stitches are needed to produce the small round pebble shapes. Quilt the first pebble in a clockwise direction, the second one counterclockwise, the third one clockwise, and so on, as shown in the diagram.

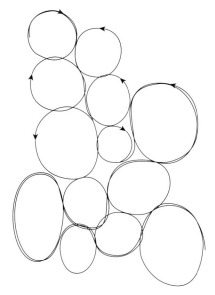

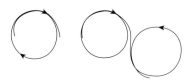

Clockwise and counterclockwise pebble quilting

To quilt pebbles on the Little Garden Cushion, rotate it so that the clamshells are running vertically. Quilt the pebbles from the top to the bottom in various sizes in a band about 2″–3″ (5.1–7.6cm) wide above the clamshells. Changing pebble size and shape adds interest to the quilting. If you are new to pebble quilting, practice for a while before working on your project.

Meandering Background Quilting

After the pebbles have been quilted, the meandering soft lines in the same color of thread in between the flowers are next. Some of the meandering lines involve spirals. When quilting a spiral, quilt into the spiral center, stop the needle, and reframe your hands before quilting out to the next spiral center. Try to refrain from moving the fabric too fast, as long stitches will look out of place.

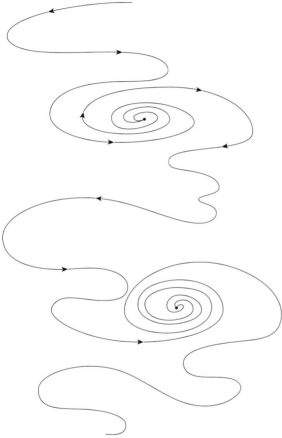

Soft-line meandering and spiral quilting

Teardrops, Oval Echo, and Pebble Combination

The background filler for the Bigger Garden Cushion and the Garden Runner is a combination of 3 similar patterns that flow from one to the other. The main idea is to have a series of fluid lines that are very small in scale to flatten the background area, complement the appliqué work, and draw attention to the decorative-stitch pattern detail. The spaces in between the vines, leaves, and flowers are very small, so a small-scale quilting pattern is needed.

Quilting a background filler on Garden Runner

■ Photo by Deborah Louie

Quilting Teardrops

Quilted teardrops are such a lovely pattern and, with a few rules to follow, they are easy to quilt. Quilt a loop, quilt a second loop in the reverse direction, quilt a third loop in the original direction, and stop. Repeat this process, counting 1, 2, 3, stop for each teardrop. The trick here is to leave the end of each loop slightly open and not touching the previous loop. You can see these small spaces in the diagram; I call them "air." Teardrops can be rounded or elongated, depending on the look you prefer.

You can plan the direction of your quilting by deciding ahead of time which side of the teardrop you want to finish on. The rule here is if the first loop travels from left to right, then the teardrop will finish on the right-hand side, which is where the next teardrop will start. Obviously, then, if the first loop travels from right to left, the next teardrop will start on the left-hand side. Knowing this, you can decide where you want to finish a teardrop and quilt it in the correct direction. This takes some practice, so start by drawing teardrops on paper. Practice quilting large teardrops to get the rhythm, and then practice smaller, tighter teardrops. The key to good stitch control with teardrops is a fast needle with slow hands and stopping after each teardrop to consider quilting direction for your next teardrop.

Basic teardrop steps

Make the loops open, not closed.

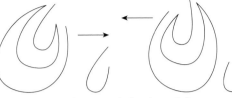

Teardrops angled right or left

Linked teardrops

Round configuration

Long configuration

Quilting Oval Echoing

This oval echoing pattern is a series of close lines starting with a half-oval shape and echoing many times around the outside, getting larger each time. As with the teardrops, the finish point of an echoed oval is the start of the next one. Oval echoes can have any number of lines, depending on how close together you can quilt the lines. If the lines are too far apart, the shape might be too large for the small space being quilted. If you finish on the right-hand side but need to be on the left-hand side to start your next oval, do another echo line.

The lines look wonderful if they are a similar distance apart, but this takes some practice. Do not connect or overlap the echo ovals at all. Leave the space or "air" between them as you did for the teardrops.

Basic oval echo steps

Round configuration with way to continuously stitch out

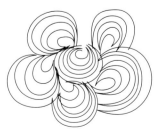

Round configuration with no way out

Pebble, Teardrop, and Oval Echo Combination

Once you are happy with each of the 3 background designs, practice quilting them together. For example, quilt 3–5 teardrops and then flow straight into 3–5 pebbles, followed by 3–5 oval echoes. Always stop with the needle down if you are feeling physically uncomfortable or unsure of what to do next.

Quilt no more than 3 square inches of area at a time, and then stop with the needle down and reframe your hands so you're ready to quilt the next small area. Continue this stop-and-go action until the background filler quilting is finished. If necessary, lift and drag the threads from one area to another when the background spaces are not continuous.

Trio of quilting patterns

 Hint: Keep checking the tension on the back of your project. Free-motion quilting usually requires a slightly tighter top tension (bigger number).

Added Magic: Quilted Tendrils and Leaves

Sometimes a small empty space, such as a small area between 2 flowers, needs a little more detail, and this is the perfect place to add a tendril or leaf. These were done in shiny black 100% polyester thread and have a relaxed free-form style.

To quilt a tendril, quilt out in one direction, stop with the needle down in the middle of a small spiral, and then return, overlapping the lines occasionally. The diagram shows some examples of this 2-step process.

Stitch the top edge of a leaf first, followed by the bottom edge, and finish with a wiggle of lines inside. Tendrils and leaves can look wonderful in different shapes and sizes throughout all the projects. Razzmatazz!

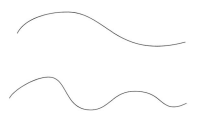 

FINISHING

—————

TOUCHES

FINISHES WITH PERSONALITY

It's fun to add a little more personality to your project with peepers, pom-poms, rickrack, and binding. Use a rotary cutter and ruler to neatly trim the edge of your project to the required size, allowing for a ¼˝ seam allowance for attaching the finishing touches, which are then sewn on with a matching color of 50-weight cotton thread in the needle and bobbin.

Peepers

The small black peepers sit next to the binding on Doreen's Place Mats and the Little Garden Cushion, and next to the pom-poms on the Bigger Garden Cushion. When made in black or a dark color used minimally in the appliqué, they act as a final frame around the project and draw out the other colors beautifully.

1. Cut 4 strips 1˝ wide × the length of each side of the project.

2. Fold the wrong sides together and press the strips in half.

3. Line up the raw edges of each pressed strip with the raw edge of the project. Stitch with an ⅛˝ (3mm) seam allowance.

When the binding is attached, ¼˝ (6mm) of the strip will peep out on the front.

Pom-Poms

I have to say, I love a pom-pom! The final effect of these delightful bundles of wool on the Bigger Garden Cushion makes me smile. Your local patchwork shop may sell pom-poms on a braid by the yard, or you can make your own. Pom-pom makers come in a range of different sizes. I used the 1⅝˝ (4.1cm) size to make the pom-poms on the Bigger Garden Cushion. The cushion has 9 different-colored pom-poms on each of the 4 sides, with a tie of wool in the same color stitched into the ⅛˝ (3mm) seam allowance before the peeper is stitched on. Skeins of 8-ply wool, tapestry wool, and embroidery wool all work well.

Doreen's Place Mat with black peepers

Pom-pom maker and wool

Rickrack

The Garden Runner has a commercial 1″-wide black rickrack attached to the edging before the binding. This scalloped look along the borders of the runner mirror the clamshells very effectively. Cut the 4 measured lengths of rickrack, one for each side, and stitch them ⅛″ (3mm) inside the trimmed outer edge. Trim away the excess rickrack for a clean, sharp edge.

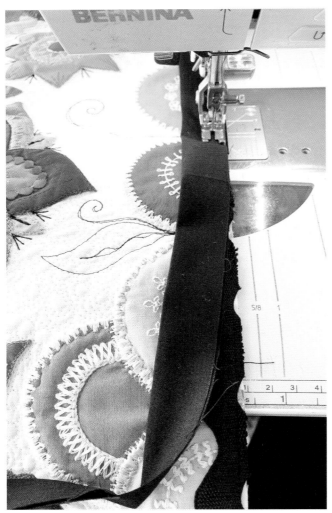

Binding being attached after rickrack
■ Photo by Deborah Louie

Binding

1. Cut the measured strips of binding fabric 2″ (5.1cm) wide and join them right sides together with diagonal seams to make a continuous strip. Press the seams open.

2. Fold and press the binding in half and attach it on top of the rickrack or peeper. Start attaching the binding to the bottom of the project with the beginning strip folded over.

3. Miter the corners as you stitch. At the end, trim the strip and tuck it neatly into the beginning fold.

4. Turn over to the back and slipstitch it in place by hand.

Beginning and ending of binding
■ Photo by Deborah Louie

Congratulations! Now you've learned all the skills you need to make any or all of the four projects. Enjoy!

—Deb

PROJECTS

Colorway Choices

Before you start any of the projects, please do not feel that you must stay with my color palette. Change the fabric and thread colors to suit your own taste. Feel free to reduce the number of colors or add more to your palette. You might, perhaps, choose your colors to reflect the decor of your home. The projects in this book are all brightly colored with a very large number of colors. They would look equally stunning with a more limited color palette.

Print fabrics can, of course, also be used for these projects. They look amazing when fussy cut in the center of the flowers and clamshells and within the individual shapes that make up the flowers. Fussy cutting is particularly effective with small-scale prints.

Please feel free to change the flowers, leaves, and clamshells in any of the 4 projects to design your own layout. If you prefer one flower over the other, use it instead. If you have made a few extra flowers, leaves, and clamshells that are not being used on your larger projects, perhaps you could use them to make a cute cushion like the Smallest Garden Cushion.

The fabric quantities for the appliqué are generous, allowing you to place your color choices in different positions to the colors in my projects.

■ Photo by Deborah Louie

Smallest Garden Cushion

Here are some projects from my very talented students. So bright and happy and, most of all, very rewarding for them to now use all the features of their sewing machines! The quilt *A Secret Garden* that greets our guests in a spare bedroom at home was the very first in this series of quilts. It was made for a QuiltNSW annual quilt show, where I was awarded a lovely ribbon in the appliqué category. I often design a major piece of work and then design smaller projects, as not everyone has the time to spend hours upon hours for months on the same quilt as I do.

The color palette here is lovely: limes, pinks, purples, grays, and black sitting on crisp white.

Little Garden Cushion by Pradnya Kanitkar

 Photo by Pradnya Kanitkar

Garden Runner by Jenny Kirk

Photo by Jenny Kirk

Detail of Secret Garden Wallhanging by Wendy Ochtman

Photo by Deborah Louie

Garden Runner by Lee-Anne Bown-Peddell

Photo by Lee-Ann Bown-Peddell

DOREEN'S PLACE MAT

FINISHED PLACE MATS: 18″ × 12″ (45.7 × 30.5cm), set of 6

Cute flower place mats are a fun way to entertain family and friends. This is the first project in the Garden series, suitable for all skill levels.

I knew the diagonal lines in the gingham check background would reveal evenly spaced quilting lines perfect for a crosshatch quilting design. You could also choose a fabric of evenly spaced polka dots or a small-scale print to provide a perfect guideline for walking-foot quilting as well.

Fancy a cup of tea, anyone?

MATERIALS

These materials will make 6 place mats.

Light gray check: 2½ yard (2.3m) for front and back of place mats

Black solid: ½ yard (45cm) for peeper and leaves

Assorted solid fabrics: ⅓ yard (0.3m) *each* of lemon, yellow, pink, coral, hot pink, and orange solids for flowers, leaves, and binding

Polyester or wool/polyester batting: ⅝ yard × 90″ wide (57cm × 240cm wide) or ⅞ yard × 60″ wide (80cm × 150cm wide)

Paper-backed fusible webbing: 1¼ yard (1.1m) × 12″ wide (30.5cm) for appliqué (I used Vliesofix Bondaweb.)

Heavyweight nonwoven stabilizer: ½ yard (0.5m) × 36″ wide (91.4cm) (I used Vilene.)

Black fusible bias tape: 1⅜ yard (1.3m) for stems

40-weight polyester thread: 1 spool of gray for free-motion stitching

40-weight shiny polyester threads: 1 spool *each* of lemon, yellow, pink, coral, hot pink, orange, and white for outside sketch-edge stitching of appliqué

12-weight 100% cotton threads: 1 spool *each* of lemon, yellow, pink, coral, hot pink, orange, off-white, and black for decorative stitching

50-weight cotton thread: 1 spool of black for piecing peepers and bindings

Bobbin fill thread: 1 spool of white for all appliqué, to be used in bobbin

Spray basting adhesive or quilting safety pins

Size 90/14 topstitch needles: 1 packet

Self-threading needles: 1 packet

Dry iron and appliqué pressing sheet

Dark, soft 2B pencil

Open-toe walking foot

Open-toe embroidery foot

Open-toe free-motion foot

CUTTING

These cutting directions are for 6 place mats. See Making the Flowers and Leaves (page 100) for the cutting instructions for these pieces.

Light gray check

- Cut 12 rectangles 20˝ × 14˝ (50.8 × 35.6cm).

Black solid

- Cut 10 strips 1˝ (2.5cm) × width of fabric.

  From 6 strips, subcut 12 strips 1˝ × 18˝ (2.5 × 45.7cm).

  From 4 strips, subcut 12 strips 1˝ × 12˝ (2.5 × 30.5cm).

Assorted solids

- From each of the 6 solid colors:

  Cut 2 strips 2˝ (5.1cm) × width of fabric for the bindings, 1 color for each place mat.

Polyester or wool/polyester batting

- Cut 6 rectangles 20˝ × 14˝ (50.8 × 35.6cm).

Paper-backed fusible webbing

- Cut 6 rectangles 12˝ × 7˝ (30.5 × 17.8cm).

Heavyweight nonwoven stabilizer

- Cut 6 squares 5½˝ × 5½˝ (14 × 14cm) for Doreen.

- Cut 6 rectangles 7˝ × 4˝ (17.8 × 10.2cm) for the leaves.

Black fusible bias tape

- Cut 6 strips 7˝ (17.8cm) in length.

Construction

Quilting the Backgrounds Before Appliqué

To make the quilting catch the eye, I used 12-weight off-white cotton thread in the needle and 40-weight gray polyester thread in the bobbin to blend with the appliqué stitching on the gray check background fabric. With heavy thread, always use a long stitch and quilt slowly to produce consistently sized stitches and to prevent drag and puckering of the 3 layers.

1. For each place mat, spray baste and sandwich together the 2 pieces of light gray check fabric with 1 piece of batting (see Basting Your Project, page 84).

2. Set up your machine for walking-foot quilting (page 85).

3. Practice on spare fabric to check your tension and stitch quality.

4. For quilting directions, see Quilting a Crosshatch Design (page 85).

5. When quilting is completed, trim the mats to 18½˝ × 12½˝ (47 × 31.8cm).

Making the Flowers and Leaves

Refer to Preparing Appliqué Shapes for Stitching (page 17) for detailed instructions. See Patterns (page 127) for the flower and leaves patterns.

You will need the following:

• Flowers: 6 Doreen

• Leaves: 18 John and 12 Roy

1. Trace and cut the shapes out of fusible webbing. Press them to the back of your chosen fabrics.

2. Cut out the fabric shapes. Stack to build the flowers.

3. Pin the shapes to the stabilizer.

Decorative Stitching

Read Decorative Stitching, One Shape at a Time (page 27) to learn how to set up your machine for various stitches, practice stitches on test shapes, and add the decorative stitching to the inside of each shape.

1. Set up your machine for machine appliqué.

2. Doreen's 5 different decorative stitches are explained in detail in Practicing Flower Doreen: Step-by-Step Guide (page 47). Draw test appliqué shapes and practice the stitches on them to choose the right stitch and setting combinations for you.

3. Choose one decorative stitch pattern at a time and, using your desired thread types and colors, stitch it onto the flowers and leaves.

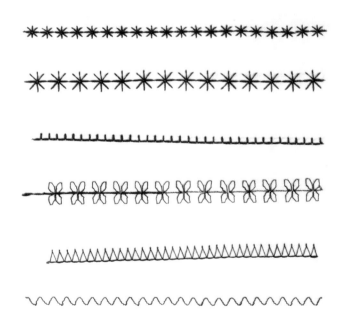

Stitches used for Doreen

4. Remove the excess stabilizer from behind all the completed shapes (see More Stabilizer Removal, page 81).

Stitches used on Doreen and leaves

Close-up of Doreen

Place Mat Layout

Refer to Project Assembly and Edge Stitching (page 63) for detailed instructions about making a layout placement pattern, placing your flowers and leaves on the background, setting up your machine, preparing and stitching bias vines, and edge-stitching the flowers.

Placing the Bias Vine

1. On each place mat, use a pencil to mark the position of the vine: 7½″ (19cm) from the top and 5″ (12.7cm) from the right-hand side edge, and curved slightly to the left.

2. Using 12-weight white cotton thread, secure the vines onto the place mats with a decorative serpentine stitch.

Adding the Flowers and Leaves

1. Place the flowers and leaves in position on the quilted background fabric. To make sure the flowers are in the same position on each background, make a placement pattern and mark the positions.

2. Press each flower and leaf in position, using an appliqué pressing sheet or a piece of parchment or baking paper on top of the project. Use basting spray if the fusible does not adhere well enough.

3. Set up your machine for free-motion stitching, using 40-weight gray 100% polyester thread in the bobbin.

4. Edge-baste the outer edges of the appliqué pieces to the background.

5. Keep the gray polyester thread in the bobbin but change the top threads to match the appliqué. Sketch-edge appliqué around the outer edge of each shape.

Finishing the Place Mats

See Finishing Touches (page 92) for directions on peepers and binding.

1. Using a rotary cutter and ruler, trim the place mats to 18″ × 12″ (45.7 × 30.5cm).

2. Prepare the peepers and stitch them onto the place mats using 50-weight cotton thread in the top and bobbin, a straight stitch with a length of 2.2–2.5, a ¼″ foot, and an ⅛″ (3mm) seam allowance.

3. Bind each place mat with a different color.

Enjoy decorating your table with your bright and happy place mats!

Doreen's Place Mat layout. You can download the full-size layout pattern and print, taping the pages together where necessary (see Patterns, page 127).

Doreen's Place Mats, set of 6

LITTLE GARDEN CUSHION

FINISHED CUSHION: 18″ × 18″ (45.7 × 45.7cm)

Here's a pretty little garden cushion to make while you learn exciting new machine decorative-stitch patterns, sketch-edge appliqué, blind hem appliqué, and free-motion quilting. Develop your skills and learn the wonderful features of your sewing machine at the same time!

MATERIALS

Sky blue ombré background: ⅝ yard (57cm) for front and backing of cushion

Light solid: ⅝ yard (57cm) for front quilt lining

Black solid: ⅛ yard (11cm) for peeper

Assorted solids: ¼ yard (23cm) *each* of 10 colors: yellow-green, yellow-orange, pink, coral, hot pink, bright green, blue-green, dark blue-green, lilac, and magenta solids for flowers, leaves, and clamshells

Polyester or wool/polyester batting: ⅝ yard (57cm)

Paper-backed fusible webbing: 2 yards (1.8m) × 12″ (30.5cm) wide for appliqué (I used Vliesofix Bondaweb.)

Heavyweight nonwoven stabilizer: 2½ yards (2.3m) × 36″ (91.4cm) wide (I used Vilene.)

Black fusible bias tape: 1⅜ yards (1.3m) for stems

40-weight shiny polyester threads:

- 1 small spool *each* of yellow, orange, coral, hot pink, bright green, blue-green, dark blue-green, magenta, white, and black for decorative stitch patterns and outside sketch-edge stitching of appliqué

- 1 small spool of sky blue for background quilting

12-weight 100% cotton threads: 1 small spool *each* of yellow, orange, hot pink, bright green, blue-green, dark blue-green, magenta, white, and black for decorative stitch patterns

50-weight cotton thread: 1 spool of black for piecing peepers

Clear polyester thread: 1 spool for free-motion ditch quilting (I recommend MonoPoly by Superior.)

White bobbin fill thread: 1 spool for all appliqué, to be used in bobbin

Spray basting adhesive: 1 can or quilting safety pins

Size 90/14 topstitch needles: 1 packet

Self-threading needles: 1 packet

Dry iron and appliqué nonstick sheet

2B pencil

Polyfill or 18″ × 18″ (45.7 × 45.7cm) pillow form

Open-toe embroidery foot

Open-toe free-motion foot

Closed-toe free-motion foot

CUTTING

Sky blue ombré background

- Cut 1 square 20˝ × 20˝ (50.8 × 50.8cm) for the top.
- Cut 1 square 18½˝ × 18½˝ (47 × 47cm) for the back.

Light solid

- Cut 1 square 20˝ × 20˝ (50.8 × 50.8cm) for the front quilt lining.

Black solid

- Cut 2 strips 1˝ (2.5cm) × width of fabric.

  Subcut 4 strips 18½˝ (47cm) for the peepers.

Polyester or wool/polyester batting

- Cut 1 square 20˝ × 20˝ (50.8 × 50.8cm).

Paper-backed fusible webbing

- See Making the Flowers, Leaves, and Clamshells (page 106).

Heavyweight nonwoven stabilizer

- Cut 1 square 20˝ × 20˝ (50.8 × 50.8cm) for the background.
- Cut the remaining stabilizer as required for the flowers, leaves, and clamshells.

Black fusible bias tape

- Cut 3 strips 9˝ (22.9cm) long, 1 strip 5˝ (12.7cm) long, 1 strip 4˝ (10.2cm) long, and 2 strips 2˝ (5.1cm) long.

Construction

Making the Flowers, Leaves, and Clamshells

Refer to Preparing Appliqué Shapes for Stitching (page 17) for detailed instructions. See Patterns (page 127) for flowers, leaves, and clamshell patterns.

You will need the following:

• Flowers: 2 Jenny, 2 Claire, 1 Rebecca, 1 Lynn, and 1 Nora

• Leaves: 8 Tony, 6 Roy, and 3 John

• 4″ clamshells: 10 full clamshells

1. Trace and cut the shapes out of fusible webbing. Press them to the back of your chosen fabrics.

2. Cut out the fabric shapes. Layer or stack to build the flowers and clamshells.

3. Pin the shapes to stabilizer.

Decorative Stitching the Flowers, Leaves, and Clamshells

Read Decorative Stitching, One Shape at a Time (page 27) to learn how to set up your machine for various stitches, practice stitches on test shapes, and add the decorative stitching to the inside of each shape.

My flowers, leaves, and clamshells had various combinations of practical, centerline, side-line, blanket, and satin decorative stitch patterns in both polyester and 12-weight cotton threads in many colors. Choose the decorative stitches from your machine that you love and will work best for you.

1. Set up your machine for machine appliqué.

2. Make practice kits by drawing appliqué shapes on fabric and adding stabilizer. Practice the decorative stitches on them to choose the right stitch and setting combinations for you.

3. Choose one decorative stitch pattern at a time and, using your desired thread types and colors, stitch it onto the flowers and leaves and inside the clamshell arches.

4. Remove the excess stabilizer from behind all the completed shapes (see More Stabilizer Removal, page 81).

Close-ups of stitching

Cushion Layout

Refer to Project Assembly and Edge Stitching (page 63) for detailed instructions about making a layout placement pattern, placing your flowers and leaves on the background, setting up your machine, preparing and stitching bias vines, and edge-stitching the flowers.

Bias Vines

The vines are stitched onto the background first. Before you stitch them, finalize the layout of all the vines, flowers, leaves, and clamshells.

1. Place the flowers, leaves, and clamshells on the 20˝ (50.8cm) background square in a position similar to the layout diagram. See the layout diagram (page 110) or design your own layout. Do not press.

2. Using a pencil, draw a smooth, slightly curved line from the base of each flower to the top of the clamshell border. Add the small offshoots for Nora and Claire on the right-hand side.

3. Remove all the appliqué shapes and set aside.

4. Press the bias vines onto the background fabric (see Preparing and Stitching the Vines, and How to Apply Fusible Bias Tape, page 66).

5. Using clear MonoPoly, secure the vines onto the background fabric with a decorative blind hem stitch along both sides of the vines (see Blind Hem Stitching the Vines, page 67).

Adding the Flowers, Leaves, and Clamshells

1. Position the appliqué shapes:

- Put the 5 clamshells on the top row, first making sure that the end of the bias strips are covered.

- Position the 4 clamshells for the bottom row so that each one is centered below the 2 clamshells above it.

- Cut the last clamshell in half and place it on the left- and right-hand sides of the bottom row.

- Add the flowers and leaves.

Press all shapes in position, using an appliqué pressing sheet or a piece of parchment or baking paper on top of the project. Use basting spray if the fusible does not adhere well enough.

2. Pin the 20˝ (50.8cm) square of stabilizer behind the top.

3. Set up your machine for edge basting (page 73), using white fill thread in the bobbin and clear MonoPoly in the top.

4. Edge-baste the outer edges of the appliqué pieces to the background. Starting at the bottom where the vine meets the flower, baste Jenny; then lift and drag to the next flower or leaf. Follow by edge-basting the clamshells.

5. Keep the white bobbin fill thread in the bobbin but change the top threads to match the appliqué. Sketch-edge appliqué around the outer edge of each flower and leaf.

6. Finish the edges of the clamshells with a heavy satin-stitch pattern to cover the raw edge (see Satin Stitch Round Balls Pattern, page 80).

7. Around the edge of the cushion, trim back the excess of the clamshells for a straight edge.

Close-up of sketch-edge appliqué on Rebecca

Removing the Stabilizer

1. Cut away the stabilizer from the reverse side of the cushion, remembering to leave the stabilizer behind the stitching (see More Stabilizer Removal, page 81).

2. Place a pressing cloth over the decorative stitching and press the cushion top.

Quilting

See Quilting Your Project (page 82) for more information about ditch and free-motion quilting and to learn how to set up your machine. Practice on spare fabric first to check your tension and stitch quality.

1. Sandwich together the completed top, batting, and the quilt lining. See Basting Your Project (page 84).

2. Set up your machine for free-motion ditch quilting. Use 40-weight sky-blue polyester thread in the bobbin and clear MonoPoly in the top.

3. Ditch quilt around all the appliqué and around both sides of the satin stitch balls on the clamshells.

4. Once the ditch quilting has been completed, the appliqué should start to pop a little. Now it is time to quilt the background fabric in between the appliqué shapes. See Background Quilting: Pebbles, Teardrops, and More (page 88).

• Using a shiny polyester thread to match the background fabric, quilt pebbles in random sizes at the base of the vines, making them smaller as you move toward the center.

• Now quilt soft floating swirls and a meandering pattern in between the leaves and flowers and up into the sky to the very top of the cushion.

5. Trim any loose or trailing threads.

Finishing the Cushion

Add the peepers and attach the back of the cushion, and you will have a cushion to enjoy.

1. Using a rotary cutter and ruler, trim the cushion top neatly to 18½˝ × 18½˝ (47 × 47cm).

2. Prepare the 4 peepers (page 93) and stitch them onto the cushion top, using 50-weight black cotton thread in the top and bobbin, a straight stitch with a length of 2.2—2.5, a ¼˝ foot, and a ⅛˝ (3mm) seam allowance. Stitch the 2 sides first and then the top and bottom.

3. Pin the cushion top and backing right sides together.

4. Starting 6˝ (15.2cm) from the left bottom corner, stitch the top and backing together with a ¼˝ (6mm) seam allowance. Stitch around all 4 sides, leaving a 6˝ (15.2cm) opening in the center of the bottom edge.

5. Use the 6˝ (15.2cm) gap to turn the cushion right side out.

6. Fill the cushion with polyfill or a pillow form and hand stitch the opening closed.

Happy days with your Little Garden Cushion. Enjoy!

Little Garden Cushion layout. You can download the full-size layout pattern and print, taping the pages together where necessary (see Patterns, page 127).

Little Garden Cushion

BIGGER GARDEN CUSHION

FINISHED CUSHION: *26˝ × 26˝ (66 × 66cm)*

*Y*ou'll love this big and beautiful garden cushion full of brightly colored flowers and leaves covered in decorative stitch patterns. It will add an abundance of texture and color to any room in your home. The addition of mini handmade pom-poms gives the cushion a fun finish.

MATERIALS

Light gray: 1⅝ yards (1.5m) for front background and front lining

Light gray small check: ⅞ yard (0.8m) for cushion back

Black solid: ¼ yard (23cm) for peeper

Assorted solid fabrics: ¼ yard (23cm) *each* of 16 colors: yellow-green, yellow-orange, lolly pink, hot pink, raspberry, bright green, dark blue-green, dark jade, light jade, lilac, lavender, purple, steel blue, cornflower blue, and sky blue solids for flowers and leaves

Polyester or wool/polyester batting: ⅞ yard (0.8m)

Paper-backed fusible webbing: 3½ yards (3.3m) × 12˝ (30.5cm) wide for appliqué (I used Vliesofix Bondaweb.)

Heavyweight nonwoven stabilizer: 4½ yards (4.2m) × 36˝ (91.4cm) wide (I used Vilene.)

40-weight shiny polyester threads:

• 1 small spool *each* of yellow-green, yellow-orange, lolly pink, hot pink, raspberry, bright green, dark blue-green, dark jade, light jade, lilac, lavender, purple, steel blue, cornflower blue, sky blue, and black for decorative stitch patterns and outside sketch-edge stitching of appliqué

• 1 small spool of light gray for background quilting

12-weight 100% cotton threads:

• 1 small spool *each* of yellow-green, yellow-orange, lolly pink, hot pink, raspberry, bright green, dark blue-green, dark jade, light jade, lilac, lavender, purple, steel blue, cornflower blue, and sky blue for decorative stitch patterns

• 1 small spool of black for stems, key-line edge, and tendril appliqué

50-weight cotton thread: 1 spool of black for piecing peepers

Clear polyester thread: 1 spool for free-motion ditch quilting (I recommend MonoPoly by Superior.)

White bobbin fill thread: 1 spool for all appliqué, to be used in bobbin

Black bobbin fill thread: 1 spool for key-line edge and tendril appliqué, to be used in bobbin

Spray basting adhesive: 1 can or quilting safety pins

Size 90/14 topstitch needles: 1 packet

Self-threading needles: 1 packet

Dry iron and appliqué nonstick sheet

2B pencil

Polyfill or 26˝ × 26˝ (66 × 66cm) pillow form

8-ply wool yarn: 1 small skein of black, green, lilac, orange, dark blue-green, bright blue, lime, yellow-green, pink, purple, coral, and raspberry for pom-poms

Open-toe embroidery foot

Open-toe free-motion foot

Closed-toe free-motion foot

CUTTING

Light gray

- Cut 1 square 28″ × 28″
  (71.1 × 71.1cm) for the top.

- Cut 1 square 28″ × 28″
  (71.1 × 71.1cm) for the front lining.

Light gray small check

- Cut 1 square 26½″ × 26½″
  (67.3 × 67.3cm) for the back of the
  cushion.

Black solid

- Cut 4 strips 1″ (2.5cm) × width of
  fabric.

  Subcut 4 strips 1″ × 26½″
  (2.5 × 67.3cm) for the peepers.

**Polyester or wool/polyester
batting**

- Cut 1 square 28″ × 28″
  (71.1 × 71.1cm).

**Heavyweight nonwoven
stabilizer**

- Cut 1 square 28″ × 28″
  (71.1 × 71.1cm) for the background
  (you might need to overlap and
  stitch smaller pieces together).

- Cut the remaining stabilizer as
  required for flowers, leaves and
  vine stitching.

Construction

Making the Flowers and Leaves

Refer to Preparing Appliqué Shapes for Stitching (page 17) for detailed instructions. See Patterns (page 127) for flowers, leaves, and clamshell patterns.

You will need the following:

• Flowers: 1 Jenny, 1 Claire, 1 Rebecca, 1 Lynn, 6 Nora, 2 Pippy, 2 Wendy, 1 Doreen, 3 Lisa, 1 Daisy, 3 Penny, 2 Lee, 1 Gail, 1 Megan, 1 Cathy, and 3 Christian

• Leaves: 38 Tony, 12 Roy, 6 John, and 4 Norval left

1. Trace and cut the shapes out of fusible webbing. Press them to the back of your chosen fabrics.

2. Cut out the fabric shapes. Layer or stack to build the flowers and clamshells.

3. Pin the shapes to stabilizer.

Close-up of decorative stitch patterns on Bigger Garden Cushion

Decorative Stitching the Flowers, Leaves, and Clamshells

Read Decorative Stitching, One Shape at a Time (page 27) to learn how to set up your machine for various stitches, practice stitches on test shapes, and add the decorative stitching to the inside of each shape.

My flowers, leaves, and clamshells had various combinations of practical, centerline, side-line, blanket, and satin decorative stitch patterns in both polyester and 12-weight cotton threads in many colors. Choose the decorative stitches from your machine that you love and will work best for you.

1. Set up your machine for machine appliqué.

2. Make practice kits by drawing appliqué shapes on fabric and adding stabilizer. Practice the decorative stitches on them to choose the right stitch and setting combinations for you.

3. Choose one decorative stitch pattern at a time and, using your desired thread types and colors, stitch it onto the flowers and leaves and inside the clamshell arches.

4. Remove the excess stabilizer from behind all the completed shapes (see More Stabilizer Removal, page 81).

Close up of sketch-edge and key-line appliqué on Penny flowers

Cushion Layout

Refer to Project Assembly and Edge Stitching (page 63) for detailed instructions about making a layout placement pattern, placing your flowers and leaves on the background, setting up your machine, preparing and stitching bias vines, and edge-stitching the flowers.

Bias Vine

The vines are stitched onto the background first.

1. See the layout diagram (page 118) or design your own layout. Using a pencil, draw a horizontal and vertical centerline on the cushion layout diagram (or your own layout) to divide it into 4 quarters.

2. Place the flowers and leaves on the 28″ × 28″ (71.1 × 71.1cm) background square, working one-quarter at a time. Do not press.

3. Using a pencil, draw a smooth, slightly curved line from the base of each flower to the outside edge. Add lines for the small offshoots to the smaller flowers as needed.

4. Remove all the appliqué shapes and set aside.

5. Using black bobbin fill thread in the bobbin and 12-weight cotton thread in the top, chain stitch the vines and small offshoot vines (page 70).

Adding the Flowers and Leaves

1. Put the flowers and leaves on the cushion background. Press all shapes in position, using an appliqué pressing sheet or a piece of parchment or baking paper on top of the project. Use basting spray if the fusible does not adhere well enough.

2. Set up your machine for edge basting (page 73), using white fill thread in the bobbin and clear MonoPoly in the top.

3. Starting at the top where the vine meets a flower, baste the flower and then lift and drag to the next flower or leaf.

4. Keep the white bobbin fill thread in the bobbin but change the top threads to match the appliqué. Sketch-edge appliqué around the outer edge of each flower and leaf.

5. Add key-line stitching (page 78) around the appliqué and to add a few tendrils. This beautifully defines the flowers and leaves. Set up your machine for key-line stitching with 12-weight black cotton thread in the bobbin. Stitch slowly around all shapes and add lines and tendrils.

Removing the Stabilizer

1. Cut away the stabilizer from the reverse side of the cushion, remembering to leave the stabilizer behind the stitching (page 81).

2. Place a pressing cloth over the decorative stitching and press the cushion top.

Quilting

See Quilting Your Project (page 82) for more information about ditch and free-motion quilting and to learn how to set up your machine. Practice on spare fabric first to check your tension and stitch quality.

1. Sandwich together the completed top, batting, and front lining (see Basting Your Project, page 84).

2. Set up your machine for free-motion ditch quilting. Use 40-weight light gray polyester thread in the bobbin and clear MonoPoly in the top.

Please note that the cushion will reduce in size to approximately 26½″ × 26½″ (67.3 × 67.3cm) after the small background quilting has been completed.

3. Ditch quilt around all the appliqué and chain-stitched vines, being careful to stitch to the side of the key-line stitching.

4. Once the ditch quilting has been completed, the appliqué should start to pop. Now it is time to quilt the background fabric in between the appliqué shapes in the light gray polyester thread.

• Quilt pebbles, teardrops, and oval echoes (page 91) in random numbers in the gray background areas in between the appliqué shapes. Lift and drag when stitching cannot be continuous from one shape to another.

5. Trim any loose or trailing threads.

Making the Pom-Poms

Make 9 pom-poms for each of the 4 sides—36 total—each with a 1″ tie of wool of the same color. I used a commercial pom-pom maker in the 1⅝″ (4.1cm) size. Follow the instructions on the pom-pom maker for easy pom-poms. Skeins of 8-ply wool, tapestry wool, and embroidery wool all work well. You also could buy commercial pom-poms on a braid by the yard.

Finishing the Cushion

Add pom-poms and peepers before you attach the back of the cushion.

1. Using a rotary cutter and ruler, trim the cushion top neatly to 26½″ × 26½″ (67.3 × 67.3cm).

2. Pin the pop-poms in place with the tails on the outside edge, spaced evenly about 3″ (7.6cm) apart.

3. Stitch the pom-poms onto the cushion using 50-weight black thread in the top and bobbin, a straight stitch with a length of 1.8–2.0, a ¼″ foot, and an ⅛″ (3mm) seam allowance. Stitch slowly, taking care not to stitch on top of the pom-poms. Once completed, stitch around one more time and, when you get to each pom-pom, stitch forward and back a few times over its tie to ensure it is secure.

4. Prepare the 4 peepers (page 93) and stitch them onto the cushion, using the same thread with a length of 2.0 and an ⅛″ (3mm) seam allowance. Stitch the 2 sides first and then the top and bottom.

5. Pin the cushion top and backing right sides together.

6. Starting 6″ (15.2cm) from the left bottom corner, stitch the top and backing together with a ¼″ (1.3cm) seam allowance. Stitch around all 4 sides, leaving a 6″ (15.2cm) opening in the center of the bottom edge.

7. Use the 6″ (15.2cm) gap to turn the cushion right side out.

8. Fill the cushion with polyfill or a cushion insert and hand stitch the opening closed.

Congratulations on completing your Bigger Garden Cushion! I hope you love it.

Making pom-poms

Bigger Garden Cushion layout. You can download the full-size layout pattern and print, taping the pages together where necessary (see Patterns, page 127).

Bigger Garden Cushion

GARDEN RUNNER

FINISHED RUNNER: 18″ × 58″ (45.7 × 147.3cm)

Make this glorious, colorful garden runner for the end of a bed, as a centerpiece for your dining table, or into a wallhanging. This stunning collection of flowers, leaves, and clamshells decorated with beautiful stitch patterns will bring springtime into your home every day. It is truly a family heirloom.

MATERIALS

White solid: 1⅞ yards (1.8m) for background (This is enough fabric for both the front and backing if desired.)

Light-gray-and-white small print: 1⅞ yards (1.8cm) for backing of runner (*optional*)

Black solid: ⅜ yard (34cm) for binding

Assorted solids: ¼ yard (23cm) *each* of 29 colors: lemon-yellow, yellow-green, citrus, yellow-orange, bright orange, baby coral, orange coral, coral, deep coral, watermelon, raspberry, baby pink, lolly pink, hot pink, raspberry, magenta, red wine, dark blue-green, dark jade, jade, light jade, lilac, lavender, purple, deep violet, plum, cornflower blue, sky blue, and black solids for flowers, leaves, and clamshells

Polyester or wool/polyester batting: 1 rectangle 20″ × 60″ (50.8 × 152.4cm) long

Paper-backed fusible webbing: 7 yards (6.5m) × 12″ (30.5cm) wide for appliqué (I used Vliesofix Bondaweb.)

Heavyweight nonwoven stabilizer: 5 yards (4.6m) × 36″ (91.4cm) wide (I used Vilene.)

Black fusible bias tape: 4 yards (3.7m) for vine and stems

40-weight shiny polyester threads:

• 1 small spool *each* of 29 colors: lemon yellow, yellow-green, citrus, yellow-orange, bright orange, baby coral, orange coral, coral, deep coral, watermelon, raspberry, baby pink, lolly pink, hot pink, raspberry, magenta, red wine, dark blue-green, dark jade, jade, light jade, lilac, lavender, purple, deep violet, plum, cornflower blue, sky blue, and black for decorative stitch patterns and outside sketch-edge stitching of appliqué

• 1 small spool of white for background quilting

12-weight 100% cotton threads:

• 1 small spool *each* of 28 colors: lemon yellow, yellow-green, citrus, yellow-orange, bright orange, baby coral, orange coral, coral, deep coral, watermelon, raspberry, baby pink, lolly pink, hot pink, raspberry, magenta, red wine, dark blue-green, dark jade, jade, light jade, lilac, lavender, purple, deep violet, plum, cornflower blue, black, and white for decorative stitch patterns on flowers, leaves, and clamshells

• 1 small spool of sky blue for stitching on bias vine

Silver metallic thread: 1 small cone for decorative stitch patterns on flowers and leaves

50-weight cotton thread: 1 spool of black for piecing rickrack and binding

Clear polyester thread: 1 spool for free-motion ditch quilting (I recommend MonoPoly by Superior.)

White bobbin fill thread: 1 spool for all appliqué, to be used in bobbin

Rickrack, 1″ (2.5cm) wide: 4½ yards (4.2m) for edging

Spray basting adhesive: 1 can or quilting safety pins

Size 90/14 topstitch needles: 1 packet

Self-threading needles: 1 packet

Dry iron and appliqué nonstick sheet

2B pencil

Open-toe embroidery foot

Open-toe free-motion foot

Closed-toe free-motion foot

CUTTING

White solid

- Cut 1 rectangle 20″ × 60″ (50.8 × 152.4cm) down the length of the fabric for the top of the runner.
- Cut 1 rectangle 22″ × 62″ (55.9 × 157.5cm) down the length of the fabric for the backing.

Light-gray-and-white small print

- Cut 1 rectangle 22″ × 62″ (55.9 × 157.5cm) down the length of the fabric for the backing.

Black solid

- Cut 4 strips 2″ (5.1cm) × width of fabric for the binding.

Polyester or wool/polyester batting

- Cut 1 rectangle 22″ × 62″ (55.9 × 157.5cm).

Heavyweight nonwoven stabilizer

- Cut 1 rectangle 10″ × 60″ (25.4 × 152.4cm) for the vine appliqué.
- Cut 2 rectangles 20″ × 60″ (50.8 × 152.4cm) (you might need to overlap and stitch smaller pieces together).
- Cut the remaining stabilizer as required for flowers, leaves, and clamshells.

Black fusible bias tape

- Cutting small offshoots first, cut as needed when pressing. Use the remainder for the center vine line.

Rickrack

- Cut 2 pieces 18″ (45.7cm) long and 2 pieces 58″ (147.3cm) long.

Construction

Making the Flowers and Leaves

Refer to Project Assembly and Edge Stitching (page 63) for detailed instructions about making a layout placement pattern, placing your flowers and leaves on the background, setting up your machine, preparing and stitching bias vines, and edge-stitching the flowers. See Patterns (page 127) for the flowers, leaves, and clamshell patterns.

You will need the following:

- Flowers: 1 Jenny, 1 Claire, 1 Rebecca, 3 Lynn, 2 Nora, 2 Pippy, 2 Doreen, 1 Lisa, 2 Penny, 3 Lee, 1 Gail, 1 Cathy, 2 Ellen, 2 Kim, 1 Denise, 1 Lozzy, 5 Jan, and 3 Eileen

- Leaves: 22 Tony, 13 Roy, 8 John, 5 Norval left, 1 Norval right, 2 Sam left, and 2 Sam right

- 3″ clamshells: 7 full clamshells and 37 half-clamshells

1. Trace and cut the shapes out of fusible webbing. Press them to the back of your chosen fabrics.

2. Cut out the fabric shapes. Layer or stack to build the flowers and clamshells. Create the flowers as you wish. Note how I altered a Kim near the center by turning the center petal over.

3. Pin the shapes to the stabilizer.

Decorative Stitching the Flowers, Leaves, and Clamshells

Read Decorative Stitching, One Shape at a Time (page 27) to learn how to set up your machine for various stitches, practice stitches on test shapes, and add the decorative stitching to the inside of each shape.

Now that the flowers, leaves, and clamshells are made, it's time to decorate them.

1. Set up your machine for machine appliqué.

2. Make practice kits by drawing appliqué shapes on fabric and adding stabilizer. Practice the decorative stitches on them to choose the right stitch and setting combinations for you.

3. Choose one decorative stitch pattern at a time and, using your desired thread types and colors, stitch it onto the flowers and leaves.

4. Inside the clamshells, stitch a variety of patterns in 12-weight white cotton thread. Take care to pivot slowly and carefully around the hand-drawn curved line.

Close-up of decorative stitch patterns on Garden Runner

5. Remove the excess stabilizer from behind all the completed shapes (see More Stabilizer Removal, page 81).

Runner Layout

Refer to Project Assembly and Edge Stitching (page 63) for detailed instructions about making a layout placement pattern, placing your flowers and leaves on the background, setting up your machine, preparing and stitching bias vines, and edge-stitching the flowers.

Bias Vines

The vines are stitched onto the background first. Before you stitch them, finalize the layout of all the vines, flowers, and leaves.

1. Press the 20″ × 60″ (50.8 × 152.4cm) background fabric.

2. Fold the runner in half lengthwise and press all the way down from top to bottom. This pressed line is your centerline guide.

3. Make a copy of the center vine pattern (page 142). Starting 1″ from the top, place the vine pattern under the background fabric, lining up the centerline of the pattern with the pressed line on your fabric.

4. Trace 1 repeat of the vine curve, and then move the pattern down to line it up again with the start of repeat 2. Continue for a total of 6 repeats.

Using the runner vine pattern (page 142), mark the vine pattern on the background fabric. The vines are topstitched onto the background first. The runner layout diagram is your guide for placement.

5. Referring to the layout diagram (at right), place the flowers in a position. Do not press.

6. Draw smooth offshoot vine lines to join the large and small flowers to the center curved vine.

7. Remove all flowers and set aside.

8. Start at one end and press the small offshoot vines onto the background fabric (see Preparing and Stitching the Vines, and How to Apply Fusible Bias Tape, page 66).

9. Press the center vine in 1 long piece, making sure to cover the start of the small offshoot vines.

10. Pin the 10″ × 60″ stabilizer to the back of the background, behind the vine.

11. Using white bobbin fill thread in the bobbin and 12-weight sky-blue cotton thread in the needle, slowly topstitch the vines and small offshoot vines (see Topstitching the Vines, page 69).

12. Remove the stabilizer from the background by cutting with small sharp scissors, leaving the stabilizer under the stitching and vine.

Garden Runner layout. You can download the full-size layout pattern and print, taping the pages together where necessary (see Patterns, page 127).

Close-up of sketch-edge appliqué on Denise and double grass stitch pattern on clamshells

Adding the Flowers and Leaves

1. Put the flowers and leaves on the runner background. Press all shapes in position, using an appliqué pressing sheet or a piece of parchment or baking paper on top of the project. Use basting spray if the fusible does not adhere well enough.

2. Position the clamshells randomly to suit your flower positions, with the half-size clamshells placed ⅛″ (3mm) away from the edge and the full-size clamshells in between them.

3. Pin the large piece of stabilizer to the back of the runner.

4. Set up your machine for edge-basting appliqué (page 73), using white fill thread in the bobbin and clear MonoPoly in the top.

5. Edge baste all the shapes.

• Starting with the clamshell at the top right-hand side of the runner, stitch all around the outside edges of the clamshells.

• Starting at the top right-hand side of the center vine and working down to the bottom, edge baste the flowers and leaves.

• Turn the runner 180° and edge baste the other side.

6. Keep the white bobbin fill thread in the bobbin but change the top threads to match the appliqué. Sketch-edge appliqué around the outer edge of each flower and leaf with the same color of thread as the shapes.

7. To finish the top edge of the clamshells, use a centerline satin decorative-stitch pattern to cover the raw edge. You could use a few different stitch patterns if preferred. See the photo of the double-sided grass stitch in My Favorite: Satin Stitch Patterns (page 41).

Removing the Stabilizer

1. Cut away the stabilizer from the reverse side of the runner, remembering to leave the stabilizer behind the stitching (page 62).

2. Place a pressing cloth over the decorative stitching and press the cushion top.

Quilting

See Quilting Your Project (page 82) for more information about ditch and free-motion quilting and to learn how to set up your machine. Practice on spare fabric first to check your tension and stitch quality.

Sandwich together the completed top, batting, and the backing (see Basting Your Project, page 84).

Free-Motion Quilting the Runner

The first stage of quilting the runner is free-motion ditch quilting with clear MonoPoly thread to stabilize the appliqué.

1. To set up your machine, see Free-Motion Ditch Quilting (page 86) and use 40-weight white polyester thread in the bobbin.

2. Practice first on spare fabric to check your tension and stitch quality.

3. Ditch quilt around all the appliqué and vines and outside the clamshells.

4. Ditch quilt inside the flowers and leaves and inside the clamshell shapes along the decorative stitch patterns. This will make the individual shapes beautifully defined and flat.

5. Once the ditch quilting has been completed, the appliqué should start to pop. Now it is time to quilt the background fabric in between the appliqué shapes with white polyester thread in both the top and bobbin.

6. Quilt pebbles, teardrops, and oval echoes (page 89) in random numbers in the white background areas in between the appliqué flowers, leaves, and clamshells. The lift and drag when stitching cannot be continuous from one shape to another.

7. Trim any loose or trailing threads.

Adding Tendrils and Quilted Leaves

1. Place black polyester thread in the top and bobbin. See Added Magic: Quilted Tendrils and Leaves (page 91).

2. Stitch tendrils and leaves randomly near the edge and in between flowers and leaves. This adds some more movement and fills in some blank areas.

3. Lift and drag threads from one to the other and trim floating threads after stitching.

Tendril and leaves added for magic

Finishing the Runner

The addition of the large rickrack mirrors the shape of the clamshells and gives a lovely finish. Stitch this down just before you add the binding. See Finishing Touches (page 92) for more details about adding the rickrack.

1. Trim the runner neatly to 18″ × 58″ (45.7 × 147.3cm).

2. Pin the 18″ (45.7cm) lengths of rickrack to both ends.

3. Stitch the rickrack onto the cushion using 50-weight black thread in the top and bobbin, a straight stitch with a length of 2.0, a ¼″ foot, and an ⅛″ (3mm) seam allowance. Stitch slowly, making sure that the right-hand side of the rickrack is sitting straight on the clamshell edging.

4. Repeat to add rickrack to the long sides.

5. Trim away the rickrack curve on the outer edge, which will be covered with binding.

6. Bind the runner with the black binding on all 4 sides. Turn and hand slipstitch the binding to the reverse side.

Congratulations—you're finished! I sincerely hope that you have enjoyed making this project as much as I did and that you have learned new skills to enjoy your sewing machine even more. Enjoy your masterpiece.

Garden Runner

PATTERNS

You can download and print all the patterns and the full-size project layout patterns from:

tinyurl.com/11436-patterns-download

Tape the pattern pages together when necessary.

Stacked Flowers

1

Daisy

2
3

Daisy

NOTE
All flowers and
leaves are shown
with individual
units reversed and
numbered.

Daisy
2

Daisy
1

Daisy
3

Doreen

Doreen
1

Doreen
2

Doreen
3

Doreen
4

5

1

2

3

Jan

Jan
1

Jan
2

Jan
3

1

2

3

4

Jenny

Jenny
1

Jenny
2

Jenny
3

Jenny
4

2
Lee

1

Lee
1

Lee
2

NOTE
All flowers and
leaves are shown
with individual
units reversed and
numbered.

1

2

3

Lisa

Lisa
1

Lisa
2

Lisa
3

1

2

3

Lynn

Lynn
1

2

3

1

2

Megan

3

Nora
1

Nora
2

Nora
3

1

2

3

Nora

Megan
2

Megan
3

Megan
1

1

2

3

4

Pippy

Pippy
1

2

3

4

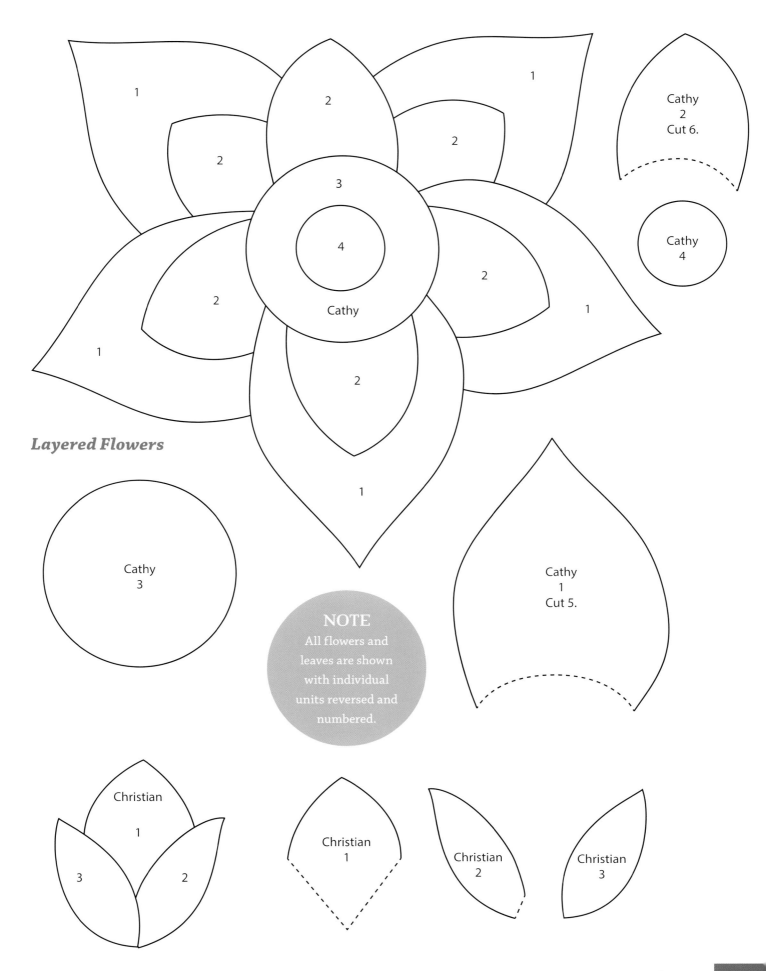

Layered Flowers

1

2

2

2

1

2

3

4

Cathy

2

2

1

2

2

1

1

Cathy
2
Cut 6.

Cathy
4

Cathy
3

NOTE
All flowers and
leaves are shown
with individual
units reversed and
numbered.

Cathy
1
Cut 5.

Christian
1

3

2

Christian
1

Christian
2

Christian
3

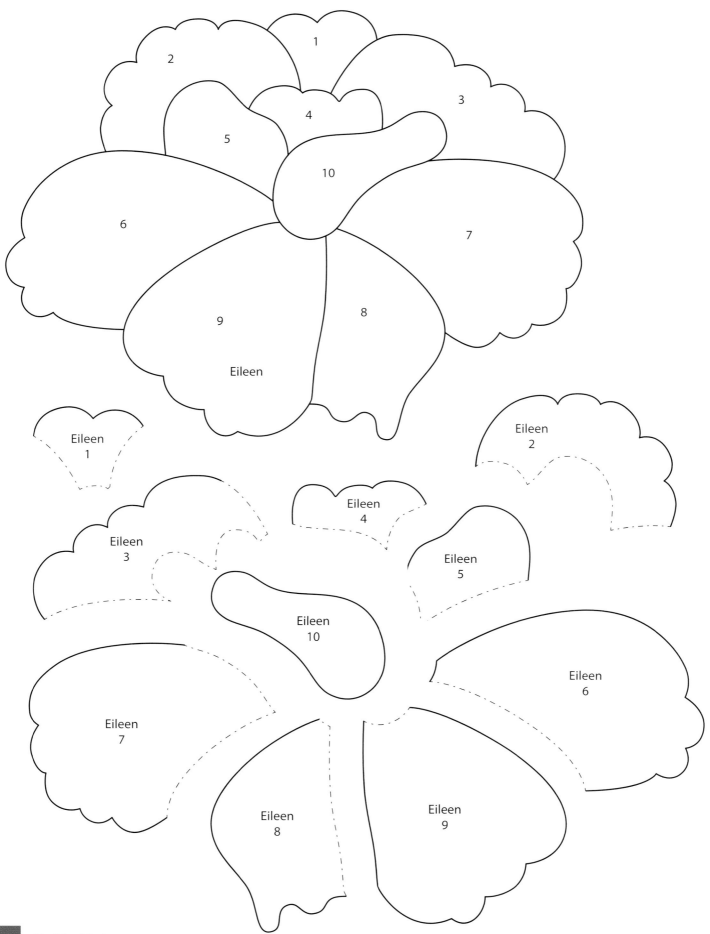

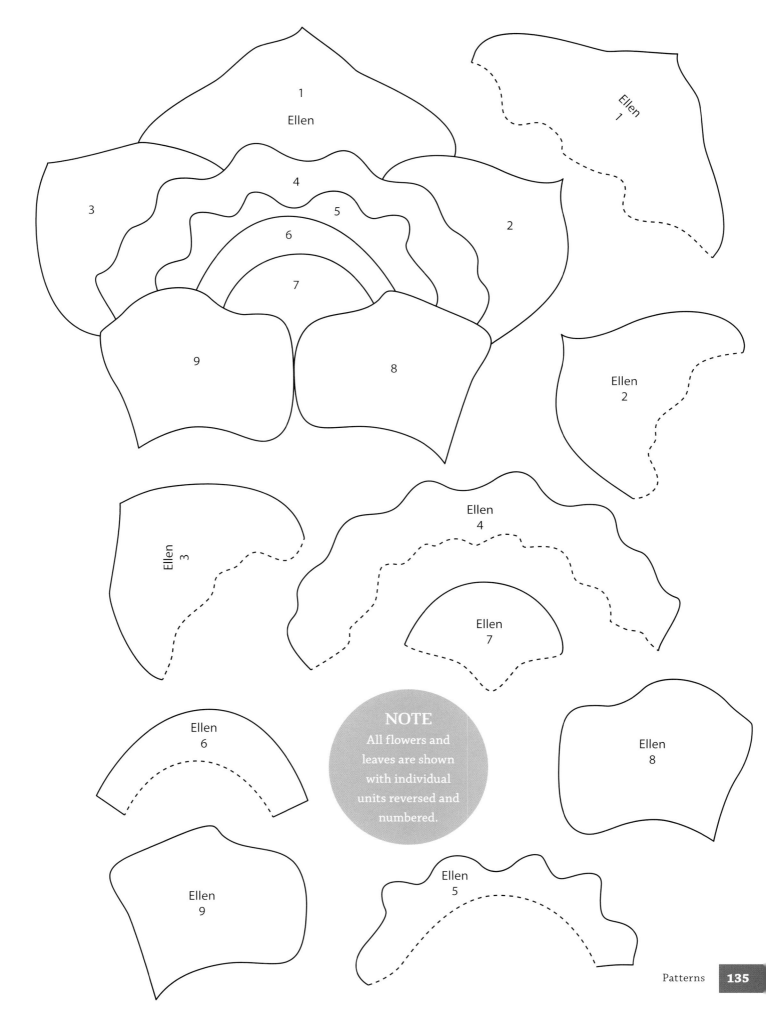

1
Ellen

Ellen
1

4

3

5

6

2

7

Ellen
2

9

8

Ellen
3

Ellen
4

Ellen
7

NOTE
All flowers and
leaves are shown
with individual
units reversed and
numbered.

Ellen
6

Ellen
8

Ellen
9

Ellen
5

Gail
1

Gail
3

Gail
6

Gail
2

NOTE
All flowers and
leaves are shown
with individual
units reversed and
numbered.

1
2
3
4
5
6
Gail

Enlarge 200%.

Kim
2

Kim
3

Kim
1
2
3
4

Kim
1

Kim
4

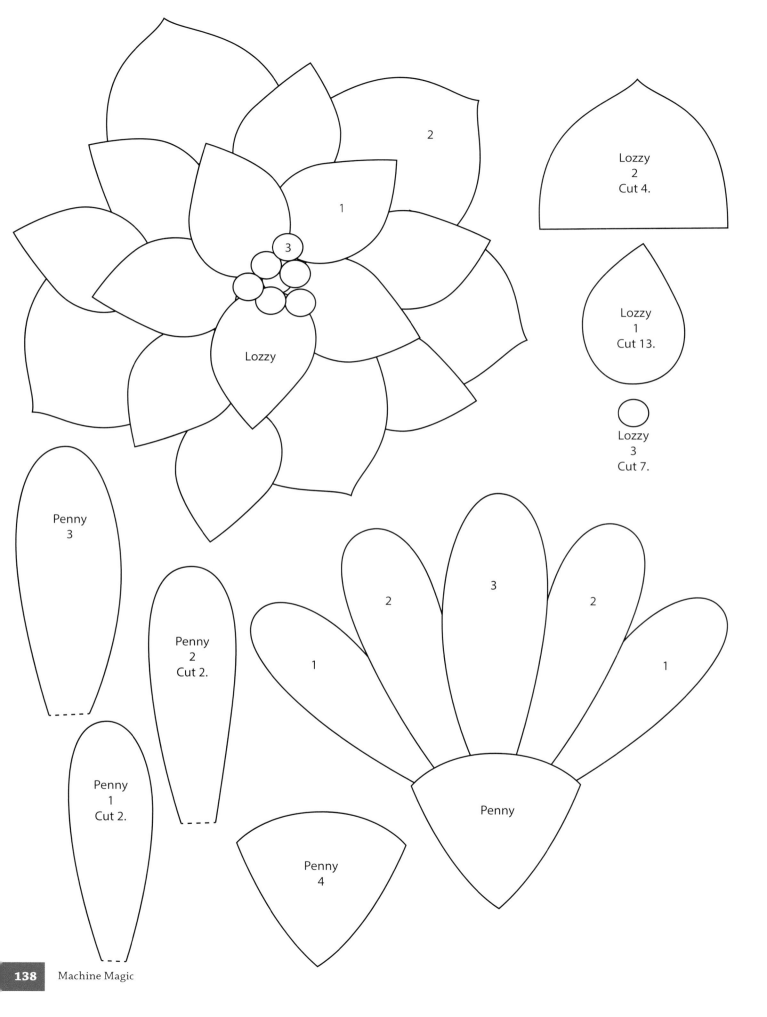

Lozzy
2
Cut 4.

Lozzy
1
Cut 13.

Lozzy
3
Cut 7.

2

1

3

Lozzy

Penny
3

Penny
2
Cut 2.

Penny
1
Cut 2.

2

3

2

1

1

Penny
4

Penny

Rebecca
1

Rebecca
1

Rebecca
3

Rebecca
2
Cut 5.

2

3

Wendy
2

NOTE
All flowers and
leaves are shown
with individual
units reversed and
numbered.

1

2

3

Wendy

Wendy
3

Wendy
1

Leaves

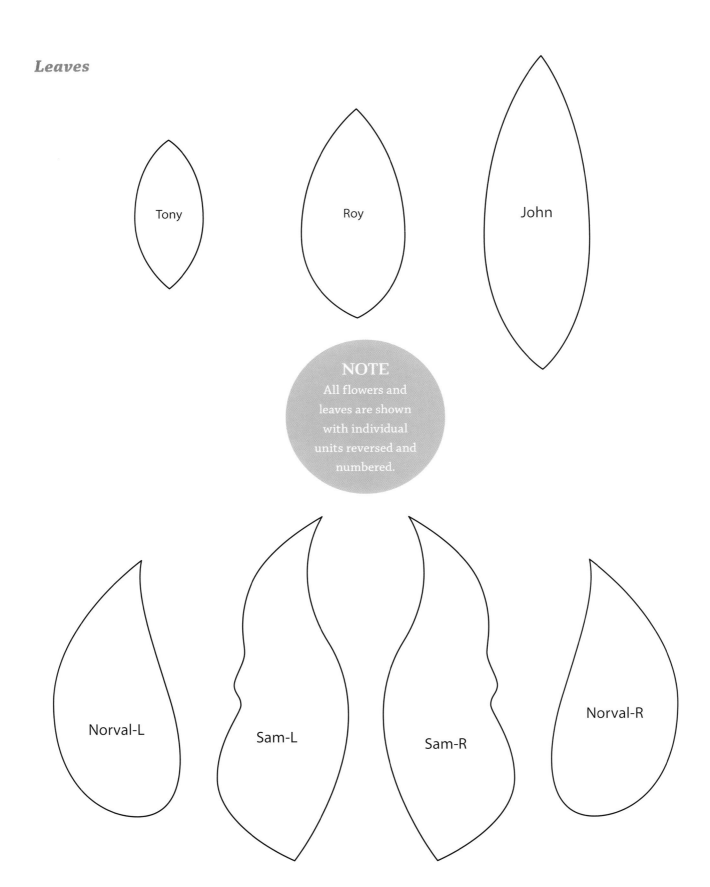

Tony

Roy

John

NOTE
All flowers and leaves are shown with individual units reversed and numbered.

Norval-L

Sam-L

Sam-R

Norval-R

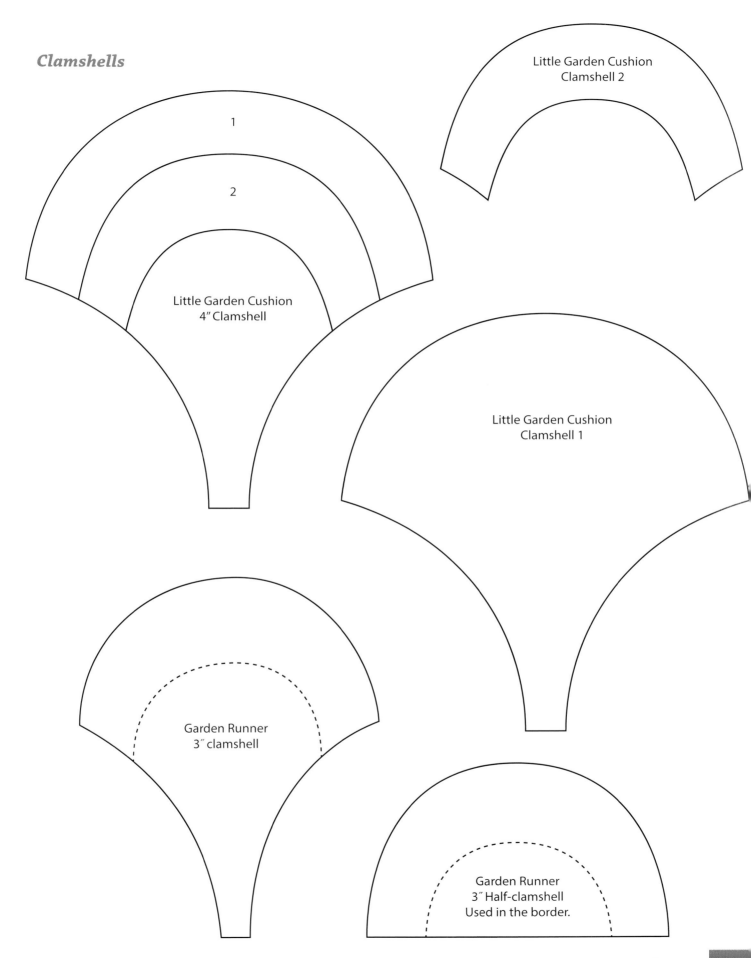

Clamshells

1

2

Little Garden Cushion
4″ Clamshell

Little Garden Cushion
Clamshell 2

Little Garden Cushion
Clamshell 1

Garden Runner
3″ clamshell

Garden Runner
3″ Half-clamshell
Used in the border.

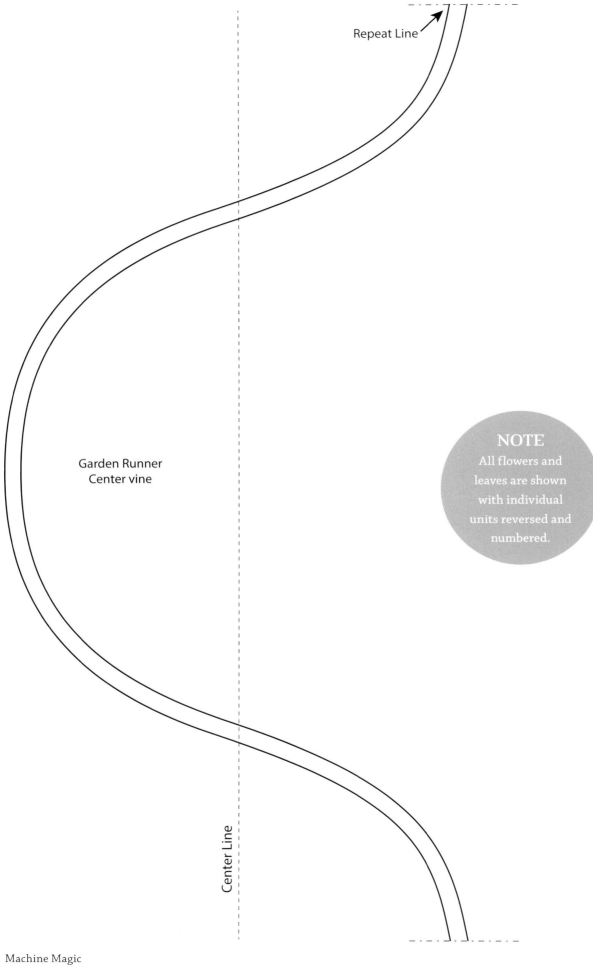

Repeat Line

Garden Runner
Center vine

Center Line

NOTE
All flowers and leaves are shown with individual units reversed and numbered.

ABOUT THE AUTHOR

Deborah's love of color, sewing, and textiles started when she was a young girl growing up in Sydney in the family textiles business, which specialized in hand dyeing laces and beautiful fabrics.

Deborah studied color and design at college before commencing work in the textile-printing industry, but her true passion was found later when she spent time at home with her young family and fell in love with quilting. Deborah started her own domestic machine-quilting business, quilting more than 600 quilts for clients. This developed her skills in both traditional and contemporary quilt design and has led her to teaching her skills and sharing her passion for quiltmaking and mastering the sewing machine.

Inspired by the river and natural bushland which surround her Sydney studio, Deborah makes unique quilts with an emphasis on color, quilting texture, and decorative-stitch appliqué. Deborah designs quilts as beautiful pieces of textile decorative art to add to your home decor.

Teaching a wholistic approach to each piece, Deborah guides students through every aspect from the design inspiration all the way to domestic machine quilting the project. Her passion for teaching others to use the beautiful features on their sewing machines shines through every book and class.

Some of Deborah's highlights include:

• Multiple award-winning quilts including first, second, and third place awards in Excellence in Domestic Machine Quilting Professional, Judges Choice awards, Machine Appliqué awards, and Best Contemporary Quilt awards.

• Accreditation as a Special Techniques Tutor through QuiltNSW guild.

• Ambassador for BERNINA Australia.

• Teaching since 2000 throughout Australia and New Zealand for symposiums, conventions, guilds, patchwork shops, Deborah Louie retreats, and groups.

• Self-publishing many skill-building books and patterns on domestic machine quilting and machine appliqué based on award-winning, original-design quilts.

• Producing online on-demand instructional classes for domestic machine quilting and machine appliqué, including "My Favorite BERNINA Features."

• Author of *Glamourous Clams*, a BERNINA Special Edition book.

• Columnist for *Quilters Companion* magazine for many years, providing advice for domestic machine quilting and machine appliqué through written articles and highly popular instructional DVDs.

Visit Deborah online and follow on social media!

Website:
deborahlouie.com.au

Blog:
deblouie.blogspot.com.au

Facebook:
/deborahlouietutor

Instagram:
@deborahlouie